Getting Stitches on a Cruise Ship

Morgan OBrien

ISBN: 9798363869822

GW00480778

CONTENTS

Dedicated to anyone out there who hears a voice in their head telling them they "can't" do something they dream of. I've heard that voice many times. It's usually wrong. Extra special thanks to my friends and supporters at Patreon. You keep this boat afloat.

- Morgan

The Introduction/ Tangent

"What do you do for a living?" is a question that I try to avoid when meeting new people. If I start chatting with someone while traveling and that question gets asked, it immediately turns into an interview... IF I tell the truth.

Actually, it's been the same way most of my adult life, even before I started producing YouTube videos. From the time I was 18 up until I turned 40, I earned my living in the live entertainment industry performing onstage and supporting backstage in theaters around the world. After the smaller summer stock and regional theater contracts, I was lucky enough to join long-run productions like "Grease!", "Ms. Saigon", and "MammaMia!".

I have a platinum album award on my wall and and a scrap book full of newspaper clippings that remind me of this former life. Each of those experiences was a dream come true, even though I learned back in my teens that showbiz is not all glitz and glamour.

That chapter ended on my own free will a few years ago, and I've traded spending my time in front of 1,500 live audience members every night to hundreds of thousands

Video editing is work I definitely have to do alone. I'm not at the earning level that I can afford to pay someone else to do it, and I'm not sure I should even if I could. Markus leaves for work at around 6:30am, I get up, fire up Final Cut Pro X, and start clicking away. No meetings, no interactions, just me and the other me on my screen.

I've tried taking my laptop to co-working spaces to at least break up the monotony of sitting at home all day and night, but the other people there are strangers who are also trying to get things done. It's not like walking into a normal office space where there's always someone to chat with about your dinner plans or the latest James Bond movie starring my ex-boyfriend, Daniel Craig. I sit alone here with the cat, who allows me to be productive when she feels like it.

(P.S. Daniel Craig is not really my ex-boyfriend. I hope you didn't Google it to see if it was true, and I certainly hope he doesn't get a hold of this book and decide to take legal action. He did ask me out several times and wouldn't take „no" for an answer. I had to block him on Instagram. He's so desperate and I could totally see him taking me to court just to be close to me again.)

Picking out the right music is a vital part of my work-flow and something that also takes a lot of time. When I get to the part of a new video where music is needed, I always have a mood or a feeling in mind that I'm trying to match. The music production service I use has a very searchable database and allows me access to thousands of royalty-free tracks for a monthly fee. I type in a few keywords, (like sassy walk or stinky fish), and start clicking through tracks. Sometimes it takes 30 minutes of listening to just a few seconds of songs at a time before I find the right one. Imagine what that would be like sitting next to me in an office, listening to 5 seconds of a song at a time for 30 minutes straight? I would hate me.

Once a video is finished, exported, and uploaded to YouTube, one of the most important steps in the entire process begins: creating an engaging thumbnail. It's like a book cover. Due to the way YouTube suggests videos to potential viewers, the way the thumbnail looks and the information presented plays a huge part in reaching new viewers, or getting existing subscribers to watch.

Deciding what goes into the thumbnail and fitting it into the proper dimensions is another really boring part of my job that takes a lot longer than people think and is absolutely not glamorous. (That being said, there is no rule against creating a thumbnail while drinking a frozen margarita on the beach in Greece, which I have absolutely done and which most people would attest is indeed quite glamorous.)

After that, I come up with a title, write a short description, select which playlists it should be added to, and I can choose where I would prefer ads to appear. I can't choose WHAT ads will appear. And did you know, even if I decide I would like to post a video with no ads, YouTube reserves the right to run ads and earn money on it? Regardless of what "I" may want? That's part of the YouTube creator experience. Keywords have to be listed, I have to digitally sign-off the content to assure it is ad-friendly, (no nudity, no major swearing, etc), and then pick a time when I want it to go online. All that is about as fun as filing your taxes, and I have to do it multiple times a week. This is the boring part that no one sees and people are very rarely interested in hearing about. Every time someone says, "Oh, you're always on vacation!" I wish they knew the truth.

Ultimately, a conversation about what I do rarely ends without the question:

"But how do you make money?"

The short answer to that question is through ads, merchandise, and mostly crowdfunding.

When it comes to earnings, being a full time YouTuber is really a roller coaster ride. Especially the income! Some unseen person, (or more likely bot), at Google sells ad space on my videos according to subject, demographic, performance, and other top-secret criteria. The better a video performs, the higher the rate can rise to run ads on it further down the line. If you are consistently uploading videos that are pulling over 20,000 views in the first week, the price is high from day one. There have been months where I've made twice my rent just from Adsense earnings. However, during 2020, there were months where I barely made over $100.

After a video goes "live", I usually know within the first few days if it's going to get a lot of attention from the outside world, or if it's reach will end with my cool club of insiders. If it gets over 2,000 views in the first 24 hours, it's a home run. If it stays under that, it typically won't end up getting more than a few thousand views before YouTube stops suggesting it to people.

I have videos that I've put several days of work into that only get seen by 1,500 viewers, and other videos that took no effort or creative input whatsoever that are seen by 500,000 viewers. It's like the music business: no matter how hard you work on something, you just never know what's going to be a hit.

I also sell the occasional t-shirt and beach towel, as well as using the Amazon referral program. If people click the link below my videos to navigate to the popular online marketplace, they help me out immensely. I don't like to mention it very often because I hate when videos seem like commercials, but I earn a commission on qualified purchases even though the price the viewer pays is the same.

The one thing that turned out to be the life boat that kept the Very unOfficial Travel Guides afloat through the stormy seas of 2020 is a crowdfunding site called Patreon. There, hundreds of unbelievably generous viewers donate money every month to support what I do. In turn, they get access to behind the scenes information, extra videos and bloopers, and other things that I don't show anywhere else.

(Ahem, no, not THAT kind of stuff… Although a very creative viewer did suggest I start an OnlyFans account with the title "The Lido Dick". I'm thinking I should reserve the URL in preparation for the next lockdown?).

There is no way I could continue to do what I do without going back to a "real-life job" without the support of my Patrons and I am so, so grateful for them. Like I mentioned, I don't get performance reviews or motivational speeches from any manager or CEO. Instead, feedback comes from the interactions I have with viewers when I'm traveling or the funny and sometimes critical comments on the videos and posts. You keep me going. Thank you to all of you.

On the following pages, I share a handful of stories that include juicy details of things I've experienced along the way. Some of them may sound familiar to many of you. There are things I have left out and certain elements that may have changed slightly since originally telling the stories, mostly because I had more time to think about the details and to talk to people who were around at the time they happened. Many of my favorite inside jokes are explained. I hope they bring a smile to your face, unless of course you are the actual "Cone Lady", who we know won't be able to smile due a recent procedure performed by her cosmetic surgeon.

Stalked by God in Israel

Just so you know, this is the only time I'm going to discuss anything religious and/or political in this book. I try to stay away from those subjects when entertaining people, but that doesn't mean they aren't important to me in my personal life. I just didn't want you to think you've gotten this far into the book before you realized I was trying to save your soul. I'm not. Throw your soul away if you like. I won't judge!

In 2010, I was nearing the end of what would be my final contract as an onstage performer in a long-run musical. I had just finished almost 7 straight years in the original German production of "Mamma Mia!", which began in Hamburg and moved to Berlin, and I was now signed on to perform in the final year of another jukebox musical called, "I've Never Been To New York", back in the same theatre where "Mamma Mia!" started in Hamburg.

The Broadway in Germany scene is huge and I had a lot of successes, which helped me pay off my student loans and put a sizeable chunk of money in the bank, but my body was giving me signs that it might be time to re-think what I was doing. Singing and dancing in musicals for all those years was literally a dream come true, but there are a lot of sacrifices you have to make, including having only one day off a week and working on every holiday.

Although I had a lot of fun in this "New York" musical, it was probably the most physically demanding show I had done, with fantastic high-kicking choreography by Kim Duddy, (who had danced for Bob Fosse and Michael Bennet back in the States.) My knees hurt, my back hurt, and it was taking me longer and longer to get warmed up for the show in order to perform at the level I wanted to deliver, which was stressing me out and giving me weird stomach aches.

Towards the end of that run, I decided to stop auditioning for other productions and give my body a rest. Fortunately, I already had a handful of videos on YouTube that were earning a couple dollars every month. I think my entire channel maybe had 100,000 views. The idea that it could become something bigger was not yet on my horizon.

When the "New York" show closed, Markus and I booked a 2 week cruise on the Mariner of the Seas leaving from the port of Civichewbaccia outside of Rome. The real name is Civitavecchia, but it's way more fun to add the wookie's name to it, isn't it?

I recently made some critical comments about the Italian city of Naples, which started a small shit storm and got me allegedly reported to the Mayor. I hope the people of Chivitavecchia who might be reading this book have a better sense of humor.

Anyways, back to the story. In addition to stopping at ports in Italy, Turkey, and Greece on this cruise, we also had two days in Israel. There, we joined up with an American family we met on board and hired a private tour-guide for our adventure.

I was raised Catholic and went to church every Sunday as well as "church school" every Wednesday night until I was 18 back in Minnesota. When I was younger, I was extremely God-fearing, so much so that I used to burst out in tears and pray for my older brother when I knew he was watching a movie on TV that our parents wouldn't have allowed him! (I'm talking normal television, where everything was censored.)

In my later teen years, as I was growing more independent and independently thinking, I realized I was going to have to distance myself from a lot of what I was taught if I ever wanted to fall in love and have a long term relationship. By the time I got to college, I had stopped going to church altogether.

I am not an Atheist and I am grateful for a lot of the values I was taught, but I also do not support the Catholic Church as an institution anymore. All that being said, getting to spend a day in Jerusalem while cruising on the Mariner of the Seas was absolutely fascinating from a religious history standpoint. I don't talk about it a lot, but it may be on my top 5 list.

Regardless of what you believe about this guy named Jesus and the miracles that supposedly surrounded him, actually being there in the settings discussed in the Bible make it all seem more real and mysterious. I spent the entire day singing songs from "Jesus Christ, Superstar".

Rami, our tour guide, took us to the Garden of Gethsemane and along the Stations of the Cross. The highlight was our visit to the Church of the Holy Sepulchre, which supposedly guards the rock on which Jesus was crucified and the empty tomb out of which he zombie-walked a few days later. This enormous, cathedral-like place is actually formed out of a few different structures that all connect together through bigger and smaller passageways.

Without our tour-guide, it would have been easy to get lost inside; that's how big it is and how many different areas it contains. After showing us the most important sites inside, Rami gave us 20 minutes to explore on our own and said we should meet him outside the entrance when we're done. Now, at this point in my life and spiritual journey, it had been more than a couple of years since I had felt close to God, but being there at the most holiest of places, (as far as Christianity is concerned), I felt compelled to take a moment and give Him/Her/Them a call.

While we were in this mega-church, I remember sitting on a random stone someplace over in a corner. I folded my hands, closed my eyes, and started the process that was a daily routine when I was a kid; giving thanks and asking for forgiveness, (a large part of my religious upbringing was centered around feeling horrible about something most of the time and begging God for forgiveness. When you are brought up that way and realize you're gay, it takes you to the bonus level of shame. Level up for hell!)

One of the things I gave thanks for was all the success I had on stage, after which I kindly asked for some guidance about what the heck I should do next. I think I asked something like, "Point me in the right direction.", or "Give me a sign." On our way back to the entrance, there was an amazing ray of perfectly defined sunlight shining from the top of the highest dome through the incense filled air that looked just like that scene in Indiana Jones where they finally find out where the Arc is.

After that, Markus and I met up with the others in our private group and made our way back out into the sunlight. Rami was waiting there and took us to a fantastic lunch spot in the old city, where we got the best falafel in a pita, smothered in hummus, as well as tangy fresh squeezed pomegranate juice. I did my best to ignore how many flies were buzzing around the juice press.

When we were finished with lunch, we followed Rami through the winding corridors of the Arabic Market. Surprisingly, it really DOES look like a scene straight out of Indiana Jones. There are vendors in every nook and cranny, selling entire pigs, scarfs, spices, (the smells are amazing!), and then the usual selfie sticks and crap like that, too. After about 5 minutes, Markus pulls me to the side.

"Have you noticed this guy behind us? I think he's following us."

I casually looked over Markus' shoulder and saw a man of about 30 years old dressed in a black suit, with black, curly hair and a black hat; the traditional costume of many men in the city. When we stopped walking, he stopped as well.

"Wait, what? Really? He looks harmless.", I said, "Should we get Rami?"

Markus took a step to the side to see if he could make eye contact with our tour-guide, and in that moment, the mystery man took a few steps towards me.

"Hello. Can I take a picture with you?" He asked, politely.

I was immediately suspicious. Who was this guy? Why was he asking for a picture of me here in this crowded market? Oh, I know! It's obviously a tourist scam! He's going to take a Polaroid of us together and then force me to buy it from him, or use it as an excuse to get us to come into his market stall. I'd been tricked like this before and thought, "Oh no, buddy. Not today!"

"Ummm, why do want to take a picture with me?", convinced I was on to his scheme, I asked him in the sassiest of tones.

"My wife and I have watched your videos about Disney World on YouTube and they convinced us to take our first trip to the United States. She's never going to believe I met you here."

MIND BLOWN

Take a minute and let that soak in. You have to remember, all of the videos on my channel at that time had a combined total of maybe 100,000 views. Even if this dude had watched all of them, he was still part of an EXTREMELY small percentage of the world who had seen my face on their computer.

I stared at him in disbelief and I think I remember hearing Markus' jaw hit the stone pathway. Of all the places that I would be recognized from YouTube for the first time, it happened THERE. Not in a theme park. Not on a cruise ship. In the middle of a crowded market in Jerusalem less than an hour after I prayed for a sign from above to tell me what I should be doing with my life.

Isn't that wild? Could it really be true that he was sent from above? The chances that one of my viewers happened to be in the same place at the same time as I was were so slim. It seems, quite literally, impossible!

In amazement, I took the picture and the man disappeared into the crowd before I could ask him his name or to get a picture myself. If Markus hadn't seen him, I would later have thought I hallucinated the entire thing.

I still think back with great amazement and confusion on that experience. It shocked me and made me start questioning my relationship to the church and my "faith." But in the end, I did not start showing up in front of the alter again on a weekly basis. Sorry, God. Don't worry, though, I did feel awful about not doing it, so at least that part of practicing Catholicism returned in full swing!

Is That a Knife In Your Bag?

I grew up outside of St. Paul, USA in the state of Minnesota. The three things that I always tell non-Americans about Minnesota is:

1) It's directly in the middle under Canada.
2) The Mississippi starts there.
3) That's where Prince was born and died.

Usually, at least one of those bits of info makes a connection for people. If it's Prince, that person immediately gets bonus points in my book. The Midwest USA, which includes Chicago, is known for having the extremest of seasons. They get tons of snow and temperatures way below zero in the winter, and in the summer, it is not uncommon for it to be over 90 degrees and about 400 percent humidity.

On one visit home for my birthday in April, (it's the 16th if you want to send me something), it was 90 degrees when I landed, and it was snowing when I left 10 days later. I am not making that up. The weather in the Midwest is as moody as a home-schooling mother of 3 whose coffee pot stopped working.

By the time I was 17, I had only been on an airplane once, and that was back in the 5th grade. It seems so strange to me now to think that I would go 17 years and only take two flights. Nowadays, things are a little different, right? I just reached the next status level on AirFrance, which makes me feel trés fancy.

Anyways, this second flight of my life was also the first time I had flown anywhere without my parents. The year was 1991 and teenage Morgan was obsessed with 3 things: David Copperfield, the Jacksons, and roller coasters.

I was a very enthusiastic member of the American Coaster Enthusiasts, which is a world-wide organization dedicated to the promotion and preservation of roller coasters. I was lucky enough to have attended one of their conventions that took place at my local theme park; Valleyfair, a few years prior. There, during another extremely muggy summer, I met with like-minded enthusiasts from around the USA to ride coasters, talk about coasters, and kindly donate about a gallon of my blood to the mosquitos on the banks of the Minnesota River.

Through my connection to A.C.E. and the friends I met during that convention, I was invited to a small get-together of enthusiasts at Six Flags Great America in Chicago. I was going to travel there the next summer to experience their brand-new Batman coaster; the very first inverted looping roller coaster IN THE WORRRRRRLD!!! (Did you hear the echo in your head?)

This coaster was a game changer and has since earned itself a place on the list of A.C.E. Coaster Landmarks. The design, which was the first coaster where riders sat UNDER the track and went upside down, is such a masterpiece that it has been cloned and reproduced at 12 other parks around the world. The original is in Great America. That was where I flew to and where I was flying home from when the incident, (that I promise I am going to get to very soon), occurred.

People tease me for my tangents when I'm trying to tell a story. But geez, sometimes you need to have all the proper information to fully understand the situation! Oh, and admittedly sometimes I just can't focus on one thing for very long. But this isn't one of those times.

Or is it?

Wait, what was I talking about?

In 1991, airports were a much different experience than they are now. You used to be able to walk through the entire airport at any time of the day, even if you didn't have a flight booked. At the end of the mini-convention, I hitched a ride with some other enthusiasts who had flights back home on the same day. I didn't have my own suitcase at the time, but I did have a blue and white duffel bag that I used as a backpack to take things to and from school and to my job at a local grocery store.

I used this duffel bag to pack the stuff I needed for this trip, but when I say "packed", I mean I just threw a change of clothes and my toothbrush on top of the notebooks and pencils and a bunch of other crap I had in there and was too lazy to remove before leaving on the trip. I'd like to say my packing technique has changed, but just a couple months ago, I was forced to empty the entire contents of my backpack at a SuperDry store and I can tell you: my passion for carrying around a ton of stuff that I don't currently need has not changed!

I got to the security check, which seems like a total joke compared to what it's like nowadays. You could leave your shoes on and have a bag full of liquids and gels if you wanted! How did anyone survive? Anyone could go into the terminal to watch you board the flight and bid you farewell. How times have changed, but you know what? Somehow airports are way more crowded nowadays, so maybe it's good that the non-traveling riff-raff hast to stay outside.

I lugged my blue and white duffel bag with it's fraying straps onto the belt for the x-ray machine, walked through the metal detector without a beep, and waited to pick up my bag on the other side. As it was coming through, I noticed the man running the operation pointing at the screen and waving for one of his co-workers to come look at something. The belt had stopped and I was the only person standing on the receiving end, so I realized they must be talking about MY bag. A few seconds later, the bag came out of the machine and a 40-something woman in a poorly fitting airport security uniform grabbed it. As she walked to a table at the end of the belt, she asked me in an accent that I, up until that point in my life, had only heard on the TV and in movies,

"This yo bag?" she asked.

"Yep." I said.

"OK, I'mma have ta search it fo security reasons."

"Ah, ok." I said.

As she ripped open the frayed velcro over the zipper and dived into the contents of my bag, I started thinking, "What could I possibly have in there that would show up as dangerous on an x-ray?" Let me remind you, this was 1991. It would be several years before liquids and gels would be no-nos. I could have had 2 huge bottles of water in there and that would have been fine.

At first, she felt around a little bit on one side of the bag, trying to be as discreet as possible, but whatever it was she was looking for, she wasn't finding it. Then she started taking stuff out of the bag. My brand new purple and black "Batman - the Ride" t-shirt. My cut off jeans shorts. (#90s) My boxer shorts, socks, a paper notebook, another notebook... I was watching her closely with an increasing amount of curiosity about what it is she hoped to pull out. Perhaps an entire floor lamp, like that scene in Mary Poppins? That would've been awesome.

She lifted up another notebook filled with old homework from pre-algebra, (and most likely a bunch of drawings involving roller coasters.) Then I saw what was underneath it and immediately broke out in a cold sweat.

Now, I'm going to have to go off on a slight tangent again but the payoff will be worth it so please stick with me.

Back in the 90s, we didn't have the internet like we do now. We had a computer at home, but it was for writing papers and playing games, it was not yet connected to all the information in the world. So, as a teenager in the 90s, if you were perhaps inclined to see what people looked like without their clothes on, as many teenage boys do, you had to somehow gain access to certain publications. Printed publications.

When you had one of those printed publications, you often traded it when you were "done" with it. You would swap with one of your buddies who had a different edition of said publication. I was one of those teenagers and I had one of those buddies. In my blue and white duffel bag, which was now spread wide open on the table at O'Hare airport was one of THOSE publications.

When I saw it, and when I saw that SHE saw it, I had a mix of feelings. It goes without saying that I was completely embarrassed. Yes, I was getting into the part of my teenager-ness where I was arrogant and felt like I ran the word and knew everything. But still I knew that I should not have that magazine and that I definitely did not want the security woman, or anyone else around me at that moment, so SEE that I had it!

(On a side note, at the same time I was also filled with a sense of joy, as I had totally forgotten about that magazine and realized it might be useful and interesting when I got back home. Sorry, that's the way teenage boys mind's work, even in situations like that.)

The security woman stopped cold. It was like a Disney animatronic that had suddenly lost pneumatic pressure. She was holding the bag open with her left hand, lifted the notebook with her right. Then, without moving her head, her eyes moved from a huge pair of glossy ta-tas up to me. She slightly cocked her head and lowered her chin, as if non-verbally trying to say, "Are you serious?" Then, with her eyes locked on mine, she mic-dropped the notebook back into the bag to cover up the contraband.

"Come ere. I wanna show you suh-im." She said as she motioned for me to move over so I could see the x-ray screen.

"Dis what we lookin fo." She said, pointing to the screen. It was a long, rectangular shaped object lighting up as bright white in contrast against the darkened outline of everything else in my bag. "It look like a knife. You got a knife in yo bag?"

I looked at the shape again and it dawned on me, "Oh, that's a box cutter! I work in a grocery store." I exclaimed. "It's probably in the side pocket, over there."

I pointed to the somewhat camouflaged zipper on the long side of the bag. "I'm sorry, I forgot I had that in there." "Look like you forgot a lot a things in yo bag…" she said under her breath as she opened the zipper. She pulled out the box cutter, which was about 6 inches long and flat. She showed it to her supervisor. Then, she pushed out all the blades into a nearby trash can and put the empty sheath back into my bag. She zipped it up, and pushed it across the table to me.

"Have a nice day." she said, sarcastically.

One question I have about this whole experience is: „Why didn't I get stopped on the way TO Chicago; only on the way back?" I definitely had the box cutter at the MSP airport. Did they not see it on the screen? Can you imagine how differently this situation would play out nowadays?

Every time I fly, I swear I see people who have no idea what to expect when they get to airport security. I don't quite understand how there can be people who haven't heard that you can't walk through a metal detector with METAL. I also don't understand how there can be people who haven't heard that you can't have a bottle of water in your carry on.

And, I don't understand why some people wait until they are standing right before the conveyor belt before they start getting themselves organised. They don't start undoing their belt and taking out their laptop, etc. You definitely can start doing that before it's your turn! Just like the people that wait until the cashier tells them how much their total is at the supermarket before they take out their wallet.

Why do people wait??? Is there a possibility you are NOT going to need your wallet? No. Is there a possibility you are NOT going to need to take off your belt before going through security? No. Go ahead and get ready sooner, people!

Missing the Boat

Before I moved to Germany in 1998, I had been working as a performer in, (and mostly out of), NYC. A few years prior, I had joined the cast of "Hello, Dolly!", at the now defunct Carousel Dinner Theater in Akron, Ohio, which was the first time I had shared the stage with people who had Broadway credits on their resume, including our Dolly; Jane White, who was Queen Aggravain opposite Carol Burnett's Princess Winnifred in "Once Upon a Mattress."

It was working with that talented group of people that led to me selling my car and beginning a long run of sleeping on people's couches in Hell's Kitchen, Spanish Harlem, Queens, etc. while auditioning for any and every show I could. Of course I had the dream of being cast in a Broadway show, but I was more or less happy to take any showbiz job that would pay my bills and allow me to do what I loved professionally.

Now you might find this hard to believe, but it's actually really difficult to find a place to live in NYC if you don't have a steady job or any money in the bank. Isn't that weird?

After I had exhausted all the couch surfing possibilities, I ended up answering a "roommate wanted" ad in a local dance studio. I've told this story on my second YouTube channel, but the guy I moved in with ended up being quite an… "experience…" to put it nicely. There were warning signs at the interview, but I was desperate to find a place to live.

After I moved in, I realized he rarely left the apartment due to bouts of paranoia that someone was following him. I discovered a hole drilled in the wall of a closet next to the bathroom that allowed him to spy on me while sitting on the toilet, (maybe that's where my obsession with Morgan-approved bathroom doors began?)

The entire situation was not cute. Around the time I moved in with "Brad", (whose name I have not changed for this story because this dude went by several names and I have no idea what his real name actually was.) I had auditioned for a production company that specialized in offering "Cirque" style of shows at a fraction of the cost of the actual "Cirque" for hotel openings, trade conventions, high-budget corporate dinners, etc.

Even though the pay wasn't fantastic, I signed on and was happy when they started sending me off on 4 and 5 night gigs around the States. Not only because I was working, but also because it got me out of that apartment! Like most people in my situation, I also had a day job handling the coat check at a very swanky steakhouse with Andi. Andi was a friend from back in the Midwest who had moved to NYC about the same time as I did. (I could write an entire other book with stories about the people who came in there and what we did with their coats.) The scheduling of these gigs for "Cirque" was sometimes very last minute and I was always very grateful for Andi, who would usually pick up my shifts.

After a few months in this situation, the production company secured a big deal to produce a gala show onboard a soon-to-be-retired cruise ship for it's final transatlantic journey.

They sent me the details, which included flying to Portugal, boarding the ship, rehearsing onboard for a week, and on the final night of the cruise, performing one single show before disembarking in NYC. As always, the money compared to the work was not impressive, but it meant over a week of not having to stay with Brad, so I was onboard with the project regardless!

There was a problem, however. The schedule at the steakhouse had already been written and there was no way Andi could cover all my shifts. I talked with my supervisor and explained the situation to her, but she was not interested in helping. I found that to be really tough at the time, but now that I'm a grown-up and have also worked in management positions, I can totally understand her. Andi and I had already switched shifts around so many times, and here I was asking for an entire week off during a schedule that had already been written!

"It sounds like a cool job and I can totally understand why you wanna do it, but if you take that job, you're gonna have to quit here. There's no way I can give you all that time off.", she said matter of factly in her New Jersey accent.

That put me in a really tough situation. I was psyched to do this very exotic sounding gig, but it meant giving up my stable day job which I was dependent on financially. Ultimately, I waited too long to give the steakhouse a clear answer and they ended up just replacing me on the schedule without even notifying me, which saved me the effort of having to write up a resignation.

I think I waited until the day before I was supposed to leave to tell my roommate; Brad. He had become very high maintenance and his behaviour was irrational and confusing.

I decided it was best to give him the least amount of time possible to create some kind of complication. He had recently threatened to start sub-subletting my room after I spent a few nights down in Mid-town at Andi's. He took the news surprisingly well. When the fly date for the gig finally arrived, I took public transportation to the airport and met up with some other performers at the gate for the first flight.

Dancers and acrobats are two breeds of humans that are easy to pick out of a crowd - especially if you are one yourself. We flew from Newark to Atlanta, where we met with others from the cast who informed us that our flight across the ocean had been delayed.

Nowadays, I would head directly to the next margarita, but back then I had different priorities and found myself sitting at the gate with another younger dancer. After another delay, I decided to find a payphone, (remember those?) to call the director of this project and let him know what was going on.

The fact that the director had his own cell phone in 1997 seemed sooo fancy to me. It may have been the first time I had ever spoken to someone who was using one.

They were flying with most of the costumes and props from Florida, and were also experiencing delays, but the plan was to stay the same until we met in Portugal.

I don't really remember much of the flight, but when we got to Lisbon, the producer and director were waiting for us at the gate. We gathered for a company meeting with others who had flown in from parts of the globe and before they said anything, I already had a strange feeling.

"Alright, here's the deal," said the producer, Nigel, through his clenched teeth. Nigel always spoke as if he was trying to hold an invisible toothpick between his molars, "we can't leave to go to the port because the ship isn't here yet. The weather is so bad offshore that it's not safe for them to navigate into the harbor. At the moment, we're still hoping to board the ship later this evening, but we're really not sure it's going to happen. I want everyone to grab a bite for lunch and bring the receipt back to Willie, (the company manager.) Try to keep checking in within the next hour in case things change, and don't leave the airport!"

Fast forward to an hour later. The weather had gotten worse and it had been decided that the ship would sail directly on to NYC without stopping in Lisbon. Nigel, who often exaggerated, informed us that he tried to rent a bunch of helicopters to fly us out to the ship, but the ship was too far away for that to work safely.

Slowly, we all came to terms with the fact that we weren't going to be boarding a cruise. Nigel informed us that Willie was already booking hotel rooms for us from the airport and he would pick up the cost of one night of hotel and our flights home.

The option to stay longer was left up to us. But we had to decide NOW because our flights were being re-booked as we spoke. Upon being asked if we were still going to be paid for the gig, even though it was cancelled, he acted annoyed. (Yet another skill he practiced frequently.)

Nigel said, "Listen, I don't even know yet if I'm getting paid for this fiasco, and if I'm not getting paid, you're not getting paid." And that was that.

Current day Morgan recognizes this wonderful opportunity to explore a foreign city with a large part of the expenses taken care of, (or perhaps read a book about cancellation clauses in contracts.)

Younger Morgan had a maximum of $250 in his back account. I had lost my job at the steakhouse for this gig. And now, due to the weather, I might not even get PAID for this job.

I figured it would be best to get back home ASAP. Current day Morgan is surprised at the level of responsibility that younger Morgan displayed in the situation. But, I'm pretty sure that if Portugal had had a major amusement park, younger Morgan would have made a different decision despite the circumstances. I spent the night in a basic hotel somewhere in Lisbon and I didn't even go out for a drink! Can you believe that? Everyone else in the cast was like, "This sucks, but let's party anyways. We're in Lisbon!", but I was like, "No! I don't have any money and now I have to call my scary roommate and let him know I'm going to be home TOMORROW. I also have to call the steakhouse and beg for my job back so I have enough money to pay the scary roommate to live with him!"

I was not in any mood to celebrate. I dreaded calling Brad. When I broke the news to him, he accused me of lying to him to confuse him. He insinuated that I was actually in NYC the entire time. He thought I was playing games with him, which made the thought of returning to his apartment even more dreadful. I did my best to calm him down, which was not easy with someone in his condition.

If I remember correctly, I was supposed to be paid $750 for the "cruise that never happened." But in the end, I wound up getting $600, which seemed like a fair compromise to me at the time. I'm positive that Nigel got paid in full and that the extra money we performers weren't getting ended up in his bank account. Willie also requested we send her any receipts we had for taxis, food, and other expenses. I never got compensated for those receipts so I know where that money went, too.

Ultimately, they did end up booking me for several future jobs, including a 4 month stint at a brand new luxury resort in Uruguay, so I guess it wasn't all bad. The ship we were supposed to sail on was the SS Rotterdam, which was retired shortly after. She was an old ship and reports say the crossing was horrible due to the aforementioned storm. I've always wondered how my relationship to cruising would have been tarnished if we had made it onboard.

What if it had been so awful that I swore to never set foot on a cruise ship again? If that was the case, you wouldn't be reading this book right now! I guess everything happens for a reason, right?

The Legend of the Cone Lady

Question for the long-time viewers of the Very unOfficial Travel Guides: Can you even eat an ice cream without thinking of this story? I'm sorry/not sorry if I have forever changed the experience for you.

Anyone who has followed my travels on YouTube for a significant amount of time knows what's coming because they either saw the first video about it back in 2014, or the subsequent mentions and re-enactments of the main character.

This took place on day 10 of my first, and to date only, trans-Atlantic cruise. (For the inexperienced out there, that's when you board the ship on one side of the Atlantic and disembark on the other side. In this case we left Miami and finished in Barcelona almost 2 weeks later, going 12 days without stopping on land.)

The ship was called the EPIC and, in addition to having a gigantic orange waterslide on top that was shaped like a toilet bowl, it also had an all-you-can-eat ice cream bar in the buffet. This counter had a small selection of ice cream and toppings with a crew member doing the scooping. While waiting in line to reward myself with some creamy goodness, (Vacation calories don't count, remember?) a woman waiting in front of me caught my eye.

Her entire appearance was something that was hard to look away from. I want to say she was in her 50s, wearing golden sandals with a slight heel, a long, flowy, somewhat sheer sundress over a bikini, several clunky golden bracelets on each arm, and large golden hoop earrings. This was topped off with a wide brimmed straw hat with, you guessed it, golden accents.

I absolutely do not want to body-shame or surgery-shame this woman, so let's just suffice to say it was apparent to even the most inexperienced of eyes that a few parts of her body had been pulled, pumped, and pushed to their limits.

The last time I saw someone wearing a pair of sunglasses that large, they were standing in the middle of a three ring circus with a curly blue wig and a bright red nose. The view of her face, top to bottom, was hat brim, sun glasses, tiny pug nose, (how did those huge sunglasses even stay up???), and the rest of her face seemed to consist of huge red lips. While I would like to give her the benefit of the doubt, there is absolutely no way she was born with a mouth that looked like that. Perhaps she had just been stung by a hornet? I don't know.

What I'm trying to say was: her lips were huge, and when she started talking to the crew member scooping the ice cream, her mouth barely moved. Her entire face barely moved. It was like she was talking in her sleep.

"Gme a scoo a runraisin, vistachio and strawvery" she muttered while pointing and clicking her long red fingernails on the glass front of the ice cream counter, bracelets jangling.

"I'm sorry, which ones?" said the crew member.

"Runraisin" click click click went the red finger nail on the glass, "Here. Zis one." she repeated.

The crew member still seemed somewhat confused, but grabbed a cup and started scooping; looking up at her to make sure he understood correctly. After the third scoop, he smilingly handed the cup across the counter to her. "Enjoy!"

The woman turned her pointing hand over, palm up. The bracelets made a jingle-jangling loudly in the process.

"No, a kooohon!" she snapped.

The dark haired crew member, once again confused, grabbed another cup, thinking he had missed part of her order.

"No! I wanded it in a KOOOHON. A KOOOHON." she spelled, "C. O. N. E! My Gaw. Why is that so hard to understahhn?"

The crew member looked defeated. He didn't understand. It was not easy to understand this woman.

A fellow passenger waiting between the woman and chimed in, "Ma'am, if you want it in a cone, you have to give him the cone. They're right there."

She helpfully pointed to one of those cone holder stands where you put the cones in a stack at the top, and at the lower end, the bottom of the first cone sticks out. When you pull a cone out of the bottom, the weight of the others on top automatically pushes the next one out into the waiting position. They were pretty common back when self-serve buffets were a thing.

Well, the "Cone Lady," (as I had already decided she was going to be called,) had obviously never seen such a complicated contraption in her life. She began trying to open it from the top and reach in to get a cone that way.

The helpful woman and I made quick eye contact and both tried not to laugh. She politely and quietly said, "Honey, just take one from the bottom. Look." She demonstrated how it works by taking one for herself.

Cone Lady then understood the process. She was already at the end of her patience, and maybe it was also the nails, but on her first attempt to hastily pull a cone out of the bottom, she ended up crushing it.

"Zheesus!" she exclaimed as half a cone went crumbling down her fingers with a crunching noise.

That's when the crew member, who had already been belittled by the woman yet still felt it was his duty to serve her, finally understood and came out from around the counter to assist her and get a fresh cone. After that, everything went smoothly.

That is the legend of the Cone Lady.

The more time I spend visiting tourist destinations, the more I realize that some people become awful when they are on vacation. For a certain type of personality, vacationing means not only leaving the cooking and cleaning duties to someone else, but leaving the manners at home as well.

Nowadays, it has become more a general description of passenger behaviour than a direct reference to that certain woman. She will always live on in my memory. I even had a t-shirt available in my merchandise store for a while in her honour. Fellow travellers write to me all the time to let me know they saw a "Cone Lady" treating someone poorly on their cruise or in their hotel and, unfortunately, it's quite common.

I've always been convinced that you can get the best customer service by being a good customer. If you ever find yourself in a situation where communication is key, stay calm and please don't be a Cone Lady!

Expensive Serum

If you want to travel the world and experience a lot of fun adventures, you have to be open to trying new things and say "yes" to opportunities when presented. Sometimes these are big opportunities that lead to amazing things. Sometimes they are smaller opportunities that nonetheless lead to something big.

One small opportunity that I say "yes" to as often as possible is the offer to try free samples in Duty Free shops. I mean, it is called Duty FREE, so go on in there and get your free stuff.

Free shot of whiskey at 6am? "Yes!" Free spray of literally any cologne on the market? "Yes!" Free slathering of the most expensive skin creams that you would never spend the money on yourself? "Don't mind if I do!"

While there is rarely a whisky tasting happening nowadays, (but I HAVE encountered them), you can always get the free colognes and creams. And that is exactly what I was doing on the way to Portland, Oregon to visit my family in the Fall of 2017.

The Hamburg Duty Free is directly after the security check. But unlike other, more modern airport designs, you can get into the gate area without actually walking through the products. The layout has not changed much at all in the 15 plus years I have been flying from northern Germany.

After threading my belt back through my pants and putting my watch back on, I navigated past the more common creams from Nivea and Neutrogena to the very back wall on the right side. That is where the good stuff is always located. The products that cost upwards of $100 for each little bottle.

It doesn't matter to me if it's from Sisley, La Prairie, Estee Lauder, or wherever, it just has to have a ridiculously high price. The cream I found on this day was in a teeny tiny little bottle and cost over $300. The name had something with caviar in it. "Golden Glow Caviar" or "Platinum Caviar Extreme" which seems insane to me. Not only insane that it probably boils down to around $12 a squirt, but if the ingredients and packaging are truly that valuable, why do they have a tester of it sitting out? That seems like a huge liability! Did someone say liability?

(Morgan enters from stage left.)

I picked up the tiny little bottle, which was about the size of a cigarette lighter, and marvelled at the ornate packaging created to transport and dispense this golden caviar. (Which, I'm sure, had exactly zero percent of gold or fish eggs inside.)

It had a shiny silver casing and a matte black pumper on the tip with an extremely small spout. When I pressed down on the top, it wouldn't move and I ended up just sliding the entire package through my hand, almost dropping it. I thought maybe you had to twist it to open it, but nope, it was solid, so I figured I just needed to press harder.

I peeled a little dried up crust off the front of the nozzle and, with my thumb below the flask, I began pressing my index finger down on the top with more force than on my first attempt. It seemed so dainty, I couldn't believe how rough you had to be to get it to work.

For a high-end product that is marketed towards rich women in their later years, it seemed wrong to make it this hard to use. I continued increasing the pressure until there was a sudden "popping" feeling. My finger sunk down on the black tip and a small stream of shiny fluid spurt out past the back of my hand and onto the wall. The tip of the spout had been clogged and, with the brute force of my finger, I managed to build up enough pressure to expel what was probably about 20% of the bottle's contents onto the wall.

It looked like a scene inside a video booth at "Peeps Show World."

Now, I think most people in this situation would have just backed away from the scene of the crime, which is probably what I should have done, too. It was very early in the day and a quick scan assured me there was no one around who had seen what happened. I could identify one sales associate close by, but from where she was standing, there was just no way she could see my creation.

I considered just trying to wipe it off with one of the tissues from the nearby cosmetic display, but it already seemed to be soaking into the coat of paint on the wall. That kind of speaks for the quality of the product, I guess? If it can melt into a coat of acrylic wall paint, imagine what it can do to your pores! I was worried I would make it worse by rubbing on it, so I decided to be a responsible consumer and not leave a disaster for someone to find later.

The sales associate I approached was about 15 years younger than me with her black hair tied tightly back into a braid. The Duty-Free uniform was form fitting dark blue pants and a blue and red striped vest on top of a white turtleneck. Something about this woman in this uniform looked "strict."

I could immediately tell she was not in a good mood, but I guess that's understandable for someone working the early morning shift way out at the airport. She probably had to wake up at 4am to get there on time. That would make me grumpy, too. Maybe she was hungover? Maybe she was just sick of her job altogether? I'm not sure, but the moment I engaged her in conversation, I immediately knew she was not going to be cool about what I wanted to tell her.

"Good morning. I've had a little accident over here. Can I show you what happened, please?" We took a few steps around the display and I pointed to the shelf where I had replaced the tiny tester.

"I was trying to use this hand cream here..." I began.

"That is not a hand cream!" she interrupted.

"OK, well, I was trying to use this cream here and when..."

"Um, that is not even a MEN'S product." she interjected again, with extra emphasis on MEN, as if the glycerin and paraffin and "caviar" in the little bottle can somehow distinguish between genders.

It was at that point that I realised my intent of doing a good deed and reporting that a clean-up was needed on aisle 7 was not going to be worth the effort. She had interrupted me twice now, and was getting louder.

"You're not interested in listening to me, are you?" I said, my tone changing from apologetic to matter of fact.

"Oh, OK. I'll listen." she snarked as she clasped her hands together below her chin like she was praying.

I tried to be friendly, patient Morgan again and very calmly started, "All I wanted to tell you was, I was trying to use this," I pointed at the product. I intentionally did not define what it was to avoid being corrected again, "and when I went to pump it onto my hand, it was clogged. So it didn't go on my hand. It went on the wall here. If you can give me a towel or something, I will gladly wipe it off."

I mean, come on. If any of you reading this have retail experience, wouldn't you say my behaviour in this situation is basically level 10 on how you would want a customer to act? Not only did I immediately report my accident, but I also genuinely offered to clean it up myself.

I thought so, but Miss Turtleneck was not having it.

"So, you just grabbed it and went `pump pump pump` into your hand???" The way she said it! It was as if I told her I had intentionally slapped my grandma. She was absolutely DISGUSTED with me.

"Well, I was trying to dispense a little onto the back of my hand and rub it in so I could test it. This is a tester bottle, isn't it?" I asked as politely as I could.

She demonstratively put one hand on her hip and pointed at the wall with the other. "These products are only here for people who are genuinely interested in buying."

Now, I am the kind of person who tries to avoid conflict. Not everyone is like that, I know. Markus really enjoys resolving conflict and, as a big boss manager in his company, he is perfect at it. That doesn't mean he goes looking for it, but when it's there, he enjoys diving into it and finding the proper way to diffuse it.

I, however, am not that way. It's not that I don't have skills and experience, but I get too emotional too quickly. If I see a conflict I can avoid, I am taking the express train in the other direction. At this moment there in the Duty Free, I was so flabbergasted by the way this sales associate was treating me. Within not even two minutes, she made me feel like I was worthless. So what did I do next? I retaliated.

"Oh, I see now. You're saying I don't look like a person who would be interested in buying one of these products. Is that what you're saying?" I asked, perhaps with a little extra portion of snark.

"If you were genuinely interested in buying, you would know that this is not a hand cream and it's not a men's product. It's a VERY EXPENSIVE SERUM."

"What if I was interested in buying it as a gift?" I smiled.

"Ah!", she exclaimed in obvious disbelief, "Really.", her eyes in a deadlock with mine.

At this point, I heard the doors of the express train out of "conflict city" open and decided to hop in. I realised there was no point in sticking around any longer, but I wanted to be sure to state my point one last time before I left. Maybe it was my Catholic upbringing kicking in from some deeply suppressed area of my brain. It wasn't that I wanted to do a good deed, it was that I needed FORGIVENESS for my sin of spilling the seed of golden caviar!

"Listen, I'm sorry that it happened, but it truly was an accident. I thought it would be a nice thing to let you know that it happened because otherwise other customers are going to come by and see this and it doesn't look nice. If you give me a towel, I will gladly help clean it off." I gave her one last chance to turn this into a somewhat positive customer experience.

"Oh no. I think I can do that myself.", she snorted.

"I hope your day gets better.", I said and removed myself from the situation.

Can we talk about what would have been a better way to handle this? If I was managing this location, what I would have expected of an associate in that situation would be something like this:

Me, "Good morning. I've had a little accident over here. Can I show you what happened, please?"

Her, "Oh my goodness, what happened? Are you ok?"

Me, "Thanks for asking, yes, nothing bad happened. I was trying to use this hand cream here and I accidentally squirted it on the wall."

Her, "Well look at that! Don't worry, I'll take care of that in a minute. It's no problem. What are you looking for today? I would gladly give you some recommendations. Are we shopping for you or for someone else?"

Me, "Oh thanks. Sorry again. I'm shopping for myself."

Her, "OK, well, these products here are our high-end products and are generally more popular with women. Should I tell you more about these, or would you like to see something else?"

Etc. If she was well trained, she would have seen the sales potential there and tried to turn the situation around instead of basically shaming me until I left empty handed. I was tempted to go buy two bottles of expensive booze and walk back past her like Julia Roberts with the dresses in "Pretty Woman".

"You work on commission, right? Big mistake. Huge."

Morgan-approved Bathroom Door

Something disgusting has creeped into hotels across the world. A plague that is growing like herpes. The more hotels I visit, the more I see cases of it in existence and I think something needs to be done about it before it gets out of control.

I'm talking about non Morgan-approved bathroom doors.

Some families and some couples are "shared bathroom" people. People who have no problem taking a shower while another member of the family is sitting right next to them dropping bombs on the toilet.

I am not one of those people and I don't understand them, either. For me, sitting on the toilet is one of the most private of duties I accomplish during the day. It is ABSOLUTELY not a group activity. I don't want to be watched or listened to while I am evacuating my bowels, and I certainly feel sorry for anyone who has to smell what remains of a Nachos Supreme after my body extracts what little nutrients were in it to begin with.

I don't get how people can have no problem with that. Which is why the trend of "show-and-tell" style bathroom situations with semi see-thru doors absolutely enrages me. I mean have you seen those barn doors that don't really close all the way, or even worse, barn doors that don't close all the way and are also made out of something semi-transparent?

Why is this happening? Who thinks it's good? I would assume if you took a poll of 100 people with the question, "Do you mind if people watch you poop?" MOST of them would say they DO mind! So who is this style for?

Up until very recently, I didn't have an answer to this question, but I've got one now and it's unfortunate.

One of my tennis partners is a project manager for hotel new-builds. I've known him for over 2 years and it never occurred to me until just a few weeks ago to ask him what's going on.

„It's all just for the visual appeal. It's a design trend that looks great on the website and on people's Instagram posts. We live in a society where form is more important than function. That's why these doors are so popular."

Ouch!

It hurts because I feel like I am part of the problem somehow. I try to imagine how the meetings go where these designs are approved.

Architect, "So, we've got a queen bed with an oak frame."

Board of directors, "Good, but we're still not convinced."

Architect, "There's a table and chairs by the window with colors that accent the walls."

Board, "OK, getting closer."

Architect, "And then I have this great idea for a bathroom door that doesn't really close all the way so that two or more people staying the room will be able to hear, smell, and from the right angle, even SEE each other pooping. BUT, they are going to be extremely photogenic."

Board, "Sold!"

When I think of the school band and choir overnight trips I did in high school where I had to sleep in a room with 3 other kids, these kind of bathroom situations would have been an absolute no-go! Can you imagine? What a nightmare. I think I want to come up with some kind of quick-fix product that you can take with you anywhere you go to remedy this problem and then pitch it on "Shark Tank".

I bet I could make millions.

Travelling with a Bodyguard

By the time I was 30, I had lived for longer than 3 months in Minnesota, Wisconsin, Florida, Illinois, New York City, Uruguay, London, Düsseldorf, Karlsruhe, Stuttgart, and Hamburg. (The last 4 are all cities in Germany).

When you work in showbiz and move around as much as I did, you meet a lot of really interesting people who are usually as crazy as you are. During the rehearsal process, you work together intensely and bond quickly. Then, when the show closes, everyone goes their separate ways and you start the process all over in a different city with a different bunch of crazy people.

Most of the time, it's very difficult to meet and become friends with people who aren't related to your job. Most people working typical 9 - 5 "real jobs" have such different schedules.

Theater people are always moving around to different shows, cities, and countries. It can be hard to keep in touch with anyone for extended periods of time. That being said, one of my closest buddies is "Kolli." (His real name is actually Andreas.)

We met in 1999 while I was working in a summer theatre festival outside of Karlsruhe, Germany. Not because we worked together, but because we were both looking for a tennis partner.

My first impression of Kolli was so awful it's really amazing that we ended up becoming great friends.

I almost didn't get into his car when he came to pick me up for our first match. (It just goes to show you that you really shouldn't judge a book by it's cover. First impressions actually CAN be wrong!)

Kolli is close to 6 feet tall and built like a rugby player. He pulled up in his slightly pimped VW Golf with Eminem blaring so loud the street was vibrating. For a moment, I thought about pretending I wasn't the droid he was looking for. But, I was desperate to play tennis, so I went through with it anyway. That choice ended up being a really great decision.

Even though Kolli works in a totally different field, his schedule jived with mine. We ended up playing tennis several times before I realised that he was just too good for me. It made no sense anymore for me to stand across the net from a player like him.

After that, we started skipping the court and just getting together for beers and movies, or whatever. By the end of that summer, we were pretty good friends and when I got offered a contract for the next season of the festival, he and his girlfriend offered to let me sleep in their extra room for the time.

Over that summer as roommates, (and the years since then,) Kolli and I have experienced a lot of fun and memorable things together. We've shared the break-ups, marriages, moves, family visits, crazy days at Oktoberfest in Munich, and even vacations of a lifetime.

If you scroll waaaaay back on my YouTube channel, Kolli was actually the camera man in my very first upload!

On a trip to California back in our 20s, the following situation occurred after flying from Düsseldorf to Frankfurt, Frankfurt to NYC, then NYC to Las Vegas. It was a ridiculously long itinerary that, fortunately, fit into our budget. We arrived in Sin City totally jet lagged. Neither of us had ever been to Vegas before and the lights of the Strip in the distance gave us enough of an adrenaline kick to pick up our rental car. Then we set out on the 4 hour drive to Los Angeles.

Yes, although we flew into Vegas, we weren't staying there until later in the week.

The first part of this adventure was filled with visits to Six Flags Magic Mountain, and Knott's Berry Farm. One of the highlights was going to the super exclusive private "Magic Castle Club." We only gained access because we were staying at the Magic Castle Hotel next door.

At this time in my life, I was signed on to the "MammaMia!" juggernaut. We had just recorded the original soundtrack, and I had been promoted to "Assistant Dance Captain." In this position, I now worked with the production team during the casting process and rehearsed with new performers.

With some of the money I got from the soundtrack royalties, I bought my first tailor made suit; a brown pin-striped number with matching Italian leather shoes. I was planning to wear it for the first time at the Club. In addition to being a huge coaster and Janet Jackson fan, I was also always obsessed with the performance of the close-up and stage illusions of David Copperfield, although I knew I didn't possess the discipline needed to present them professionally.

I can go onstage to sing and dance for thousands of strangers and know instinctively how to improvise and cover up any small mistakes. But with card magic, for example, you either do it or you don't. I can't handle that kind of pressure!

The best of the best come to the Magic Castle, which opened in a former private mansion in 1963. Magicians use this venue to try out new material and hone their craft. I was thrilled to take a peek inside the walls of this legendary location.

I'm also sure that if it wasn't for my enthusiasm, Kolli would never have considered spending the money we spent on dinner and drinks in that legendary place.

While I had gone all out to look like a superstar, Kolli had chosen a rather conservative all black suit and tie. (To tell you the truth, I think we were probably both wearing the only suits we owned at the time.)

When we were met by the hostess of the evening, (who's name I unfortunately can't remember, but let's call her Mary,) Kolli stayed a few steps behind to avoid being engaged in small talk in English. This was only his second visit to the USA and he was still dealing with a bit of culture shock and some major jet lag. I had made the reservations and knew what the deal was, so it just made more sense that I did the talking.

"Hello and welcome to the Magic Castle!" the very enthusiastic Mary chimed, "You're our friends from Germany I see! Do you work in the magic industry, or what brings you here to us?"

"Well," I took a deep breath, realising I had just been presented with a fantastic opportunity to talk about myself. It's a favourite pastime of people in the musical world. "I currently work for LittleStar and Stage Entertainment on the premier production of ' MammaMia!' in Hamburg. I don't perform magic, but I've reached a stage in my career where I'm successful enough to be able to come here and support these artists, and I'm thrilled to see what they have to offer."

"Well fantastic!" she said, "We are so happy to have you. And what about you? Are you a fan of the magical arts?" she asked, turning to Kolli.

Kolli looked confused for a second, then managed to say, "I'm chust here becauszse of him."

"Great! Follow me." chirped Mary as she led us to the dining room.

The Magic Castle was formerly someone's private home, but it's rooms have been repurposed into a restaurant, a few bars, and several performance spaces ranging from intimate parlours to a small theatre with curtain, proscenium and the whole shebang.

For non-members, (most of which are company outings,) a visit to the Castle always includes dinner, which we definitely would have skipped if we could have. At that age and time in our lives, I'm pretty sure it was the most expensive meal I had ever paid for out of my own pocket. For some strange reason, I can remember Kolli had seafood pasta, but I have no idea what I had.

Once dinner is finished, the performances begin on a rotating schedule. There were so many artists performing that Mary informed us we wouldn't be able to see all of them. Desperate to milk this evening for all it was worth, I had looked at the schedule and made a plan about how we could see most of them.

We arrived at the first venue to see a guy named Joshua Jay. He was a well known up and comer who at 25 had already written two popular instructional books. I had heard about him and was excited to be able to see him in person, but when we got to his room, every seat was already full. Seeing his show first was important for my plan to be successful, but it looked like it wasn't going to happen.

I stood there, disappointed, which caught the attention of Mary, who was waiting to introduce the performer.

"Don't worry," she told us, "Wait here. I'll be right back."

She left the room and returned a few minutes later with 2 chairs, which she set up at the end of an already very tightly packed row. Then she asked a few people to change seats so that the end was free for both of us.

I thanked her profusely for her trouble and was kind of embarrassed that there was such a fuss about us in front of all the other guests. But I was happy to be in the front row for Joshua's amazing show. One of the highlights I remember was his „ambitious card" trick, where a randomly selected and signed card keeps jumping to the top of the deck, even after it is obviously buried in the middle.

Joshua also had a great spin on the old classic where he gave someone sitting in the audience a TV remote and made that person press "channel up" every time the card was supposed to jump to the top. After a few fantastic jumps, however, he started fumbling. The card got lost and he seemed to have failed at finishing the trick. Then, in a masterful plot-twist, he said, "Wait a second, maybe it's not me that's off, maybe it's the remote. You've been pressing up, right?", he asked the audience member.

"Yep. Every time." she replied.

"Strange. Well, the card is not jumping to the top anymore. I think it's the remote that's stopped working. Let me ask you. What do you do when you're watching TV at home and the remote stops working?", Joshua asked, slyly.

"I check the battery," she replied.

"Exactly." He smiled, "You've had that remote in your hands the entire time, correct?"

"Oh my God shut uuuup!", the audience member said, already foreshadowing what was to come.

"Open up the remote and tell me what's in there." And of course, it was the SIGNED CARD!!!

I love shit like that. That feeling of being totally dumbfounded by something you know can not possibly be true, yet every bit of input the universe is giving you says otherwise.

Another famous magician and author, Paul Harris, says that people like to watch magic shows because, for a short moment of time, it makes us feel like little kids again. Our minds are forced to create a new category for an event we have not yet experienced, which happens less and less the older we get and the more of the world we get to know.

Watching Joshua Jay teleport a signed card into a remote control in the middle of the audience turned out to be only one of the highlights of that evening.

After Joshua's amazing show, Mary appeared and made a bee-line for Kolli and I.

"What did you think? Isn't he amazing?" She bragged, then asked, "So guys, where do you want to go next?"

I told her that we had planned to see the next showing in the main theatre, where a husband and wife team were presenting some large scale illusions. We had about 20 minutes before the show started and were thinking about grabbing a drink.

"Alright, follow me, I'm going to get you a seat right now." she said and scurried off. This seemed odd to me. I mean, at maximum capacity, only about 500 people fit into the entire mansion, but still.

I thought to myself, "Doesn't she have something more important to do?" On the way there, she tried to make small talk with us, but I did most of the talking and Kolli avoided getting involved with the conversation. He was not used to speaking English in this kind of a situation and was much more comfortable being a silent observer.

She walked us directly into the theatre, which was more or less empty.

"You guys grab any seat you want, how about right here?",she said, pointing towards the front and center in the first row.

"Thank you so much! We'll take a look and grab a seat in a second." I said.

"Well, if there is anything I can do to help, you just come find me, ok?"

I was confused. How was she able to provide this level of service to all 500 guests? Was there more than one Mary?

Not long after the stage show, Kolli's jet lag got the best of him and he decided to go back to the hotel. It was only shortly past 10 pm. Although I was also very tired, I wanted to get the most out of this possibly once-in-a-lifetime experience.

After one more round of shows, the "official" venues closed and the remaining guests of the night were welcome to mix and mingle with the artists in one of the bars. If you're lucky, you might get a private show.

While standing in line to get a seat at one of the tables where a slight-of-hand artist was showing his skills, an older gentleman walked directly over from the bar. The gold pin on his lapel identified him as a club member.

"Hello, I wanted to introduce myself. I'm Michael and I'm one of the long-time members of the Magic Castle. You're our guest from Germany, right? Are you enjoying yourself?" he inquired.

"Yes, this is something I've been looking forward to for a long time." I answered.

"That's fantastic. We are so happy to have you here. If you need anything, you just let me know. Can I bring you something to drink? Do you want me to introduce you to any of the performers?"

"Oh, thank you so much. I'm just going to hang out a little bit and then hit the road. It's been a long few days." I said.

"Well, anything you need, you just let us know."

"Thank you so much." I replied.

Once again, I began to get suspicious. I didn't see random members of the Club offering to get the other guests drinks. This dude was not hitting on me. He just seemed genuinely interested in making sure I was having a good time… but why me? He went back to the bar and I noticed him say something to the bartender, who then looked surprised and shot a look back over at me. What was going on?

After watching the small show over the shoulders of some guests, I decided to grab myself a drink. Unfortunately, I had paid for dinner with cash and didn't have enough money left in my wallet to order anything on the menu, so there I was, in my tailored pin-striped suit and $300 Italian leather shoes quietly asking for a free glass of ice water when another group of people approached me.

"Are you Morgan?" said a tall woman in a stunning evening dress. Her long, blonde hair was slicked back and I could immediately tell by the way she was standing with flat shoulders and a long neck that she had spent several years at the ballet barré.

"Eh, yes." I said.

"Mary told us that you work with Littlestar in Europe and we just wanted to say hi. We're all dancers." she gestured to the 3 men she was with, all tall and fit, with perfectly styled hair and bright white LA smiles.

"Ya!", I exclaimed, "I'm in Hamburg working on ' MammaMia!' at the moment." I said, once again thrilled to have received an invitation to brag about myself.

"Are you the choreographer?" one of the guys asked.

"No, but I work with the associate choreographer during the casting and rehearsal process, and I'm also a swing in the show, so if enough people are on leave or injured, I perform as well."

"That sounds amazing! Congratulations on booking that gig." the woman said.

"Ya, that sounds awesome." One of the smiley guys chipped in with a Latin accent, „Hey, where's your bodyguard? Did you send him home?"

"My WHAT?" I asked, genuinely puzzled.

"That guy who was with you. Wasn't that your bodyguard?" he asked again.

"No!" I exclaimed, „Who said he was my bodyguard?"

I could tell by the reaction of the woman that my response came off a little too defensive. I was just so surprised by the question that it must have sounded snippy when it came out of my mouth.

"No no no, honey. Nobody said he was your bodyguard…" she said, gently putting her hand on my shoulder, "…but we heard you were an actor from Europe. And you have this big dude with a shaved head in a black suit following you around all night and not saying anything. I think everyone here just kind of put two and two together."

I mean, it does make total sense when you look at it that way. It immediately became clear to me why we had been getting all that special attention. Remember, this was the early 2000s. It would still be a couple years before everyone had a device with high-speed internet in their purse, and "Googling" someone was not really a thing yet.

Just like my new dancer friend said, the people in the Castle had assessed the situation based on face value and had come to that conclusion. "This short guy from Europe in an immaculately tailored suit is apparently so important that he travels with a bodyguard."

We definitely fit the description!

"Oh my gosh! Noooooo!", I laughed, the long drawn out "oooo" sound giving away my Minnesota roots. "We're just friends!", I explained.

I spent the next hour chatting with this fun group of fellow stage professionals. Having formerly danced in a big review in Vegas, the woman was able to give me a lot of tips for our upcoming visit that turned out to be really useful. When I finally went back to our room, Kolli was still awake watching American television. I explained to him what happened and he was just as surprised and entertained as I was. Nowadays, it's a joke that comes up at least once every time we get together.

On a side note. When we were in Vegas, two of the most well-known magicians, Sigfried and Roy, were still performing their groundbreaking show at the Mirage. For some reason, we skipped it in lieu of getting discounted tickets for Cirque du Soleil's "O."

I knew how legendary the German magician's show was and figured I would be back in Vegas sometime and put it high on the list then. Unfortunately, just a few months after our visit, the show would close due to a "misunderstanding" between Roy and one of his white tigers. I will always regret not taking advantage of the opportunity to see that milestone in magic, showbiz, and Vegas history.

The Jolly Joker

Alright, I feel like this story needs a disclaimer, so here goes. When it comes to the "party" scene, I was a very late bloomer compared to most people I know. I did not experiment with alcohol or weed in highschool, even though I knew people who regularly used both, and even harder things. I waited until I was 21 to have my first cocktail, (with a great group of friends in Stevens Point, Wisconsin.) I never even got drunk enough to have a hangover until a few years later on tour with a children's theatre production of "Swiss Family Robinson."

Not until I moved to Germany when I was 24 years old did I start to consume alcohol on a semi-regular basis with friends on the weekends. I never smoked weed until I was in Amsterdam's famous Red Light District, where it is completely legal and somewhat regulated. Call me a party pooper, but I don't think you should be drinking alcohol if you are underage, and you probably shouldn't be smoking weed at all, especially not where it's illegal.

Due to certain circumstances in my younger years, I just was never really interested in smoking pot. For me, drugs were drugs, and I had seen what other drugs did to people. I was not interested in becoming one of those people. Even though I was an adult and had seen a lot of the world, from many not so pleasant personal experiences when I was younger, I just assumed drugs made you lazy, lose control or act like an asshole. It wasn't until I was comfortable in my career and sexuality, had my own apartment and money in the bank that I finally felt like I might be interested in trying it out. I wanted to be sure that I wasn't missing anything in life that I could possibly end up turning to drugs in order to compensate.

"Grease!" had closed in Düsseldorf and I was commuting to the nearby city of Oberhausen to perform in a less than

stellar, yet big budget, production of "A Christmas Carol."
Andi, (from the steakhouse coat check in New York),
contacted me out of the blue and said she and her friend
Mark wanted to visit me in Germany and take a trip to
Amsterdam.

Since the last time I had seen her, Andi had landed some
big gigs on Broadway and I was really excited to get
together again and catch up. Mark was someone I had
heard a lot about, but never met. He and Andi went to
college together and his career led him to Hollywood,
where he had already been in some very well-known
movies and TV series.

The couple of days we spent together in Düsseldorf were
filled with a lot of laughter and nonsense. Both Andi and
Mark are fantastic comedians and willing to do anything to
make each other lose it. We made up new rules for
Scrabble, played Uno, tried to record our voices backwards
and then play it back forwards to see if we said things
correctly, etc. Just fun stupid stuff that was free and made
us laugh. I had shows most of the time they were visiting,
but there was a 2 day break in the schedule on which we
planned our drive over to Amsterdam.

After we checked into our hotel, (with Morgan-approved
bathroom door,) we celebrated by opening a bottle of
sparkling wine. I think it was included in the price of the
room. I have a picture of me holding a glass in one hand
and for some reason have a shower cap on my head. On
that first night, we made our way out into the city. Our first
order of business was to find a cozy looking coffee shop
where the two of them were excited to be chaperones on
my inaugural journey to the Emerald City.

Andi and Mark had more experience in mind altering
substances than I did, (yet still became extremely
successful, which debunked my theory at the time.) I felt

safe being with them. Just knowing THEY knew what they were doing gave me the sense of security that I needed to overcome the inner fears I had about the whole thing.

I assumed I was going to take one drag on a joint and immediately my world would change in ways that would have me questioning reality. I was worried they were possibly going to have to prevent me from jumping into the canal. Or that they might have to convince me that there were no pink elephants marching down the street. In hindsight, I was very naive and ill-informed about the actual effects of marijuana!

The red light district of Amsterdam is fascinating. There are narrow, winding streets as well as wide open passageways surrounding the canals, (which are basically water streets). Coffee shops abound, as well as fast food places where you can get french fries in paper cones, doused in mayo and piled high with chopped onions.

Just like the name says, there are red lights everywhere. Red lights mark the windows where there are prostitutes in business. These are mostly unbelievably beautiful young women who rent a small room with a window directly out to the street. If you are interested in spending some time with them, you approach their door and negotiate a price for services. Then, she turns off her light after you enter her lair to "complete the transaction." None of us had ever seen an area like this and we were all fascinated.

After poking our heads (and noses!) into a few coffee shops that didn't have the vibe we were looking for, we eventually found ourselves in the city's Nieuwmarkt area in front of a corner shop called the "Jolly Joker." It was less full than others we had passed, with a large window looking out on the street. It also had a cool little upper balcony with only one table that I thought would give us some privacy for my upcoming out of body experience.

If you've never been to a coffee shop like this, the whole experience is very similar to going to a Starbucks. Well, except for the penetrating smell of ganja in the air. There's a counter with one or two people working behind it. There are muffins and sandwiches to buy, as well as soft drinks and coffee.

Then, usually on a separate menu laying on the counter, is the selection of the pot. You can buy it in little bags, in pre-rolled joints mixed with tobacco, or you can buy the so-called "Space Cakes" to eat instead of smoke. I remember being surprised at how normal that atmosphere felt inside. Part of me was really disappointed that it didn't feel somehow more underground and "naughty."

By the time we had ordered and got up to our table on the second level, I'm sure I was already buzzing from the second hand fumes. However, the amount of adrenaline in my blood from just being there and my worries that something horrible was going to happen must have been enough to cancel it out.

As I set up a Scrabble board that I grabbed from a nearby bookshelf, Andi and Mark lit up the pre-rolled marijuana cigarette. I felt a moment of very high anxiety when it was passed my way. I thought, "This is going to change your life forever, Morgan. Maybe this isn't a great idea. What if you get so high, you can no longer tell what's real???"

Andi reminded me again that one doesn't usually hallucinate from smoking pot, but that I definitely should only try it if I really want to. They would not be disappointed if I didn't. She also reminded me that she has had many more horrible experiences involving alcohol than she has ever had involving pot.

So, in a final moment or resolution, I lifted the joint to my lips and attempted to inhale just a teeny tiny little bit of smoke. I wanted the equivalent of taking a tiny sip, not downing the entire shot.

There was a strange taste on my tongue and I felt a slight dry feeling in the back of my throat, but the immediate shift of my mind into a different transcendental plain did not happen. The tiles in the floor didn't start to melt and bend. I couldn't feel the colors with my hair. I didn't immediately want to eat an entire bag of chips. All the crazy things I expected to happen the split second after puffing did not appear.

"I don't feel anything." I said. Andi and Mark, trying to be patient with me and my unfounded anxiety, reminded me again that the feeling you get from getting stoned is different than drinking and that I shouldn't expect anything major to happen.

They both took another turn on our joint and then passed it back to me again. Mark said, "Let me watch you do it. Maybe you just aren't getting any smoke. In order to really get the benefits, the pot has to burn. That burning turns into smoke, and that smoke has to get into your lungs. Breathing it in gets the chemicals into your blood, which then makes you feel stoned. Watch me once." He sucked hard on the little white rocket, "You see how the end got red? That's how you know it's burning."

He passed it to me. "OK, watch." I knew I wanted to get it right, but I also didn't want too much. I had never smoked a normal cigarette, either, and was unsure about the proper mouth and lung mechanics needed to inhale the smoke without going too far. I held my lips tightly around the paper end and did what I thought I needed to do.

"Nope. Nothing." said Mark. "You really have to suck for a second, either into your mouth, or deeper."

Now, frustrated with my inability to master what millions consider a simple task, I decided to just go for it. I exhaled as far as I could, put the joint between my lips and sucked in HARD.

"There ya go!" exclaimed Mark.

After what was probably only around 2 seconds, I immediately started violently coughing and handed the joint back to Andi. She and Mark laughed and pushed my ice tea across the table to me.

"Geez, take a drink, stoner." said Andi, jokingly. I laughed and coughed as tears streamed down my face and my nose started to run.

"That's some good shit." I managed to mumble; quoting the movie "9 to 5." The two of them, with their excellent comedy skills, found it highly amusing to act overly embarrassed by my coughing fit. They actively made eye contact with anyone they could in the area below us and mouthed, "We're so sorry!" They gestured melodramatically in my direction, "He's gonna be ok."

My coughing and laughing spell continued and I started to notice an increasing burning sensation in my throat and chest. Mark went downstairs and bought me another cold ice tea, which helped soothe this uncomfortable feeling somewhat.

After a few minutes I still couldn't take more than a few normal breaths without violently coughing again, which worried me. Remember my paranoia that something bad was going to happen, even before I smoked?

Queue the dramatic music!

Slowly, I started to lose the feeling in my finger tips. At first, it was just a slight tingling, but then my hands started to cramp so that I was involuntarily making fists. This was, of course, alarming, and made my heart beat even faster, causing me to breath even faster, which was causing me to cough even more again.

"Are you OK?" asked Andi, looking somewhat startled.

"I," cough cough, "I think I just need some," cough, "fresh air." I choked out the words and when I stood up, the edges of my vision started to blur and darken. I could see the door down the small flight of narrow stairs and was intent on getting out into the street before I spontaneously combusted, (or whatever was about to happen.)

"I'll come with you," said Mark.

When I finally made it out of the smoke-filled Jolly Joker, the cold December air smacked me in the face and felt fantastic in the inside of my nose. Mark was nice enough to grab my jacket on the way out and handed it to me while I sat down on the curb. I couldn't open my hands enough to put it on, so I cuddled it like a baby. He sat down next to me.

"What's going on? What's wrong? Talk to me." he said.

At this point, I'd like to remind you that I didn't really know Mark. I knew he was a college friend of Andi's and that we had had a good time in the few days prior to this night. Otherwise, my only reference of him was in the movies and TV shows he had been in… and did I mention that he usually plays the villain? He is a very sweet, charming dude, but he looks like a bad guy.

I started speaking a mile a minute, "I don't know. My lungs are burning. And," cough cough, "my throat. I can't feel my fingers. Look!" I showed my fists. "I can't move my fingers. I feel like I can't breathe." At this point, I was in full panic mode, and more or less panting. Deep breaths hurt, so I was compensating by taking many short breaths. Too many.

What I needed at that moment was someone to tell me, in a very matter of fact tone, something like, "OK, you are hyperventilating. Your lungs are burning because of the deep drag you took. That will go away in a few minutes. You just need to take some normal, calm breaths and let your system reset. Then your hands will relax and you will start to feel more normal. This happens to a lot of people the first time they smoke a cigarette or a joint. You're going to be fine, but it's going to take another minute or two."

Like I said, that is what I would have LIKED to hear. However, instead of that, I turned to Mark who, in my paranoia and the neon lights of the Red Light district, suddenly looked like the MAXIMUM villain possible (for a person not wearing prosthetics, of course.)

He attempted a soothing voice, but in my state, he sounded more like the Joker. "No man. It's just a new energy. It's good energy. You just need to let go and let it take over. You'll see."

I was immediately convinced he was out to get me. My mind raced. Could I run away from him? Push him away? No. Play it cool. Don't let him notice you're scared.

I gathered enough air to say in one breath, "Mark. Ummmm. Do you think you could go back inside and ask Andi to come out here for a second?" I managed, though I was still coughing and my voice sounded like a little boy's. When he stood up, the muscles on the back of my neck tensed up as he crossed behind me.

In the few minutes that passed before Andi got to me, I had managed to breathe enough of the cold air in regular cycles to even out my blood oxygen levels. My hands were beginning to un-cramp as Andi explained that the joint was a mix of marijuana and tobacco. She told me it was most likely my body reacting to its first shot of nicotine that was causing my heart to race and my lungs to burn. She saw I was shivering and helped me put my jacket on as she apologised for not thinking of that in advance. "We should have given you some without tobacco for your first time. Sorry about that." she said. These were the things I needed to hear.

After about 15 minutes, I was feeling more or less normal again, and we went back inside. It seemed like every soul inside that small shop was staring at me as I climbed back up the narrow stairs to our second level table. The paranoia was real, but maybe they actually were?

I didn't smoke any more that evening. We went out to dinner at a somewhat fancy restaurant and I remember thinking it was the best food I had eaten in a very long time, if ever. I wondered how you could make "mustard soup" so tasty. And the crunchy croutons on top! The way they got soft in my mouth when mixed with the sour warmth of the soup was a process that fascinated me. I wanted to do it over, and over, and over, and over. I ordered a second bowl before my main course arrived.

I was definitely stoned.

After that first experience, you may be surprised to hear that I did actually smoke again before the week was over! We went to a new place and used a different technique and it went much more smoothly, although I was still puzzled as to why there wasn't a noticeable change in my mood or the way the world seemed.

There are very few similarities between the feeling of smoking marijuana and drinking alcohol. After the little experience I had with it, I could understand why there are so many people fighting for legislation to legalise it's use back in the USA, especially for medical reasons. But I was also happy to try it when I was in a good "place" in my life, both literally and figuratively.

I can't believe how many young people start experimenting with alcohol and drugs in high school. With all the hormones and mood swings and self consciousness, it seems like the worst time to put yourself through that!

Lake of (bad) Dreams

This is the only story in this book that happened in my home town, but it's got a similar tone as most of the other stories, and I've never told it to you before, so I figured now is a good time to share it.

About a 30 minute bike ride outside the city of Hamburg is an old sand quarry that is filled with water. It's more or less in the middle of nowhere and it would be really hard to stumble upon if you didn't know it was there.

The first time I ever visited the "Boberger See", (which means Boberger Lake in German), was on a 2nd date with a guy I had met at an underground dance club inside an old, burnt down theatre. I can't believe I just wrote that, but that is literally where I met Bart.

Bart was a tall, lanky, thin-rimmed glasses wearing grade-school teacher who looked like he used to skateboard. I chatted him up at the club and we had a great conversation. Realising we were both vegetarian, he made the next move and invited me over for dinner. I went to his place the next Monday night, (this was during "Mamma Mia!" times, so I only had Monday nights off.) Even though he was an absolutely TERRIBLE cook, we still had a great conversation.

While trying to digest the unseasoned steamed artichoke petals with plain sour cream dip he served for the main course, he talked about growing up on a farm and how he loved the outdoors. I talked about spending time at my grandparents house on Long Lake in Wisconsin and also spending a lot of time outdoors.

He said he became an elementary school teacher because he loved helping kids, and that he wanted to be a father. I told him that I also wanted to be a father. I told him I had ridden over 400 roller coasters around the world. He showed me his on-ride pictures from the local amusement park.

The list of things we had in common became very long and as the evening was drawing to a close, he asked if he could show me his favorite "nature" place outside of Hamburg. He then described the lake in the quarry way out in the middle of nowhere, (which, at the time, sounded fantastic to me, but now that I wrote it down, warning bells go off!) We agreed to meet early that Wednesday to make the trek out there.

Yes, you read that correctly: I did not spend the night. I went home with a big smile on my face like a good Catholic boy should. It was a tough decision because I was really into him at that point, but it would have made what happened next even worse.

As I mentioned, the lake is a nice bike ride outside of the city. Because it was forecast to be in the high 80s, Bart suggested we take our bikes on the train to get a little bit closer, then only ride the last few miles. He also insisted on packing a picnic basket for both of us, which made me cringe thinking of his culinary taste and abilities. I was still trying to impress him at this point, so I agreed.

I actually didn't have a bike of my own at that time. But a fellow cast member had a big green monster of a bike she let me borrow while she was out of town, and it currently was locked up outside my place.

The day arrived and we left early because I had to be back in the theater that night at 6:30pm. I think we met at 9am, (which is really early for someone who works nights.) We made it out to the train stop by around 9:30am.

With the hot sun beating down on the back of our necks, we carried our bikes down the stairs of the single-platform train station and made our way across the German countryside. Past farm fields with horses grazing. Into the woods, following a path along a large stream. In the cool areas from the shady trees, there were swarms of mosquitoes. I felt like I was back in Minnesota. We pedalled on. Over a small bridge to the other side of the stream, close to a road. We passed a small parking lot; the last sign of civilisation before crossing the stream one more time. After biking about another half a mile on a dirt path with the stream on our left side and a barbed wire fence on our right, containing a herd of grazing cows, Bart stopped.

"So, this is the tricky part.", he said. "We have to lift our bikes over the fence, and then we go under."

"Wait, what? Really? Are… are you sure? What about all the cows?", I said. Being confronted with the challenge of pushing my bike through a field of cows was not something I remembered reading in the description for this particular excursion. "Isn't there another way?" I asked.

"There is, but it takes much longer. Come on. It'll be fine. This is how I always go. Wait," he asked with genuine surprise in his voice, „Are you scared of the COWS?" His inflection was like he had just found out I had never tasted ice cream in my life. As if it was absolutely shocking that I was hesitant about throwing my (friends') bike over a barbed wire fence into a field of gigantic, free roaming animals.

My mom also grew up on a farm and told me horror stories of being chased by a bull, so I knew that not all cows are friendly. I was scared, but from the way Bart got closer to me, I realised there was something about it he found very cute, which may or may not have led to me ham it up a bit. Also, the fact that he was not afraid of these potentially vicious future-steaks made him seem very masculine to me, which was an instant turn on.

We dodged the barbed wire, walked through the cows, who couldn't care less that we were pushing our bikes through their food. We did the same thing with our bikes and the fence on the other side of the field. Following a dirt path through more trees, we eventually ended up at the lake.

Except for a small patch of sand on the opposite side from where we were, this body of water was almost completely surrounded by trees. It really did look like a lake of dreams and I was stoked. We turned right and, after another short stretch through a wooded area, came to a large clearing where several other people were already setting up blankets and claiming their spots for the day.

It wasn't a place that everyone knew about, but it also wasn't completely abandoned. We picked a spot towards the edge of the field where the low grass turned into high grass, spread out our blanket, plopped the picnic basket at the edge, (Bart really did have an old-fashioned picnic basket), and went for a swim.

One detail I haven't mentioned yet because it's not actually that relevant is that most of the people hanging out on this field next to the lake were butt-naked.

The nudist culture in Germany actually dates back to the late 19th century. In many public pools and parks, there are dedicated nudist areas, and if you go to a spa with a thermal suite kind of area, 95% of the guests will be naked. The other 5% are people from other countries and they stick out like a sore "insert name of body part here."

By this point in my life, I had been to nude beaches and spas and it really wasn't a big deal for me. It also carried the extra added bonus of letting me see more of what Bart had to offer as a partner, (which turned out to be as disappointing as his cooking, but wait; there's more! Stick around. This story gets worse. Much, much worse.)

After a round of swimming and slowly slathering each other's backs with sunscreen, we popped open the picnic basket and Bart and I snacked on cheese cubes and handfuls of dried granola. Yum!

"This is such a nice day and you are such a nice guy and I am so happy we met.", Bart started, "I called my brother yesterday and told him all about you, and he's happy for us, too." His brother still lived on the farm and Bart was proud of how cool his hillbilly brother was with him being gay. "He can't wait to meet you. And I was thinking, we could spend Christmas with my parents this year, and then go to the USA next year from Christmas."

Please keep in mind, this was the middle of the summer, we were on our second date, and all the sudden he's making Christmas plans. It seemed so absurd, I genuinely thought he was kidding.

"Ya, right", I laughed, „and we better start picking out bridesmaids dresses soon."

His smile grew. "Really???", he asked.

"No, not really! I'm kidding. What are you talking about, Bart?" I said, sitting up.

"I just thought it would be nice if you met my family. They're excited to meet you.", he said, shrugging his shoulders.

71

"Woah, dude. Slow down. We literally just met a week ago. I mean, I like you, but let's not make Christmas plans yet." I was trying to sound charming, yet firm.

Bart turned his head towards the water, where an older couple were helping each other out of the water. The man was on the banks of the lake, reaching down to give his wife a hand. She pulled too hard, he lost his balance and fell back into the water; his side slapping the surface as he tried to avoid landing on top of her. They laughed. I laughed. Bart exhaled loudly.

"Ok. Fine." He said, sounding pissed.

"Listen man, I really like you and we have a lot in common, but let's plan next week, not next year. We've gone out on two dates and maybe they'll be more, but geez, let's take it step by step."

He sat there quietly for about 30 seconds, then he slammed both hands down on the blanket and quickly stood up.

"I need to go for a walk. Alone."

"Allllllright," I said as I watched his skinny, naked white ass walk quickly towards the water.

That was the moment I decided that this relationship was not getting a callback.

I sat there for a few minutes, devouring as many cheese cubes as I could before he came back. He had also brought a bottle of wine, but I had to work that night so there was no popping the cork and slamming a glass of chardonnay. It was a very tempting thought, given the circumstances.

I improvised several possible conversations in my head in anticipation of his return and eventually ended up laying down on the blanket and staring up at the deep blue sky, listening to the wind blow through the tall grass behind me.

A few minutes later, he returned and started violently slamming things back into the picnic basket without saying a word. I asked politely, "Um, are we leaving?"

"Well I'M leaving", he said, „and honestly, I could care less what you do."

Now, this is going to sound very insensitive of me, but at that moment, I burst out laughing. It was our second date! We chatted in a disco, had dinner, and now we were on our way to divorce court. I really liked him up until that point, but this was too much.

"Okayyyyy then. Goodbye, I guess?" I said.

Bart quickly pulled on a pair of shorts, haphazardly attached the picnic basket to the luggage thing on the back tire of his bike, and made a large circle around the blanket, (that thankfully I had brought), to head back the way we came.

"Unbelievable!" He yell-whispered, still within earshot. I did a double face-palm and laid back down on the blanket, shaking my head.

Remaining in that position for a while, I started analysing the conversations we had to try to come up with any kind of foreshadowing moment where I should have seen something like this coming. I tried to think of what I could have changed to avoid this outcome because he seemed like a really great guy, but this behaviour here at the lake was unexplainable to me.

After probably about 10 minutes of just laying there, I decided to stop worrying about it and try to enjoy another hour or so at this calm, beautiful place before heading back to the city, but there was a problem: I didn't know the way back. At no point in our journey to the lake did I consider we might not be returning together, so I didn't pay a proper amount of attention to what path we were on or which direction we were going. I had a mobile phone at the time, but it would still be a few years before we had the internet and maps on those kinds of devices.

I tried to trace our steps back in my head, but kept drawing blanks around the small parking lot. Eventually, I decided I could just follow someone else. There were about 50 people on this field by now and I was sure someone would be leaving around the time that I left and I could just watch where they go and follow behind until I saw something familiar.

Up until this point, I was also sitting there in my birthday suit, but I was feeling a little insecure after the whole ordeal and decided I wanted to put on a pair of swim trunks that I had in my backpack. Everyone around me was naked, so I figured it was better to move to a place where there were other clothed people to not be one of "those" people at the nude beach.

Following the path along the water, I found a small clearing surrounded by trees and bushes that had a path directly to the water's edge. It was like a natural "cabana", and it gave me pretty much complete privacy, which was what I was looking for at that moment. I threw the blanket down, let my backpack plop off my shoulder, and laid my borrowed bike sideways on the grass. Not completely trusting the situation, I took my wallet out of my bag and hid it under the blanket, which turned out to be the best decision I made all day.

Then, I hopped from the rough bank into the cool water and went for a swim to ceremoniously wash off the bad energy of the last hour. I made a few loops, swam out into the sun, treaded water a bit, and looked back to the path I came down.

While out in the middle of the lake, I remember thinking, "Why can't I just meet someone normal?" In hindsight, I'm sure a lot of the guys (and girls, for that matter,) I had met that I never called again thought the same thing after meeting me.

When I started swimming back to my cabana à la nature, I thought I saw someone thru the trees, but I figured he was also looking for a place to chill and moved on when he saw my stuff already spread out. I got back to the place where I had jumped into the water and realised that my legs were too short to get back up on to land. The bottom of the lake is a very soft sand, but the banks are muddy and gritty. I would have had to use at least one hand and a knee in the mud to get back up, so I opted to swim a little bit over to where Bart and I had entered the water because I knew I could get out there fine.

When I got back to my stuff, I had a moment of confusion because I was sure I had zipped up my backpack before I went swimming, but now it was wide open. I shrugged it off, picked up my nice, scratchy towel, and dried off. By this time, it was already well past noon, and I figured if I wanted to go home before going to the theater, I better start packing up because who knows how long it was going to take me to find my way back to the train station.

Remembering that one of my cast mates had told me he had been to this lake before, I thought about calling him to ask if he could guide me in the right direction. I reached into my backpack to take out my phone, but it wasn't there. After about 30 seconds of frantically searching every corner of my bag, I confirmed that my phone was no longer in my possession and that it must have been stolen. Back then, there was no such thing as a flat-rate. You paid for every minute you talked, and if the person who stole my phone decided to call Japan, for example, that would be a huge bill.

I knew I needed to act fast. In a slight panic, I ran back over to the main field where there were other people and started the casting process for the role of "Most Likely To Let Me Use Their Phone."

Two young guys laying on the same blanket immediately got the job because I figured we would have the gay thing in common and they might be more willing to help. I tried to approach them calmly.

"I'm sorry to bug you and I know this is going to sound like a scam, but I'm sitting over there," I gestured towards the bushes, "and while I was swimming, someone just stole my phone. Would it be ok if I use one of your phones to block my contract?"

Surprisingly enough, one of them agreed without hesitation and I quickly dialed the easy-to-remember helpline for my contract. The fact that someone immediately answered shows you how long ago this took place. The whole process took maybe 2 minutes until my phone was blocked and; as a polite gesture, I offered the guys free tickets for "Mamma Mia!"; which was sold out for the next few months.

"Nah. Thanks. We're good." One of them said. This made me realise they were very obviously NOT gay! I thanked them again for helping me out and walked back down the path to my stuff.

Except now there was less stuff. My entire backpack was gone.

I know many of you are screaming at the page right now. It seems so obvious that I SHOULD have taken it with me when I went to find someone to help me block my phone, but at the moment, it never occurred to me.

I figured the bad guys (or girls, or non-binary thieves of a different gender) had already gotten what they wanted. I flung the blanket up by one corner and was happy to see that my wallet was still there and sat down on the grass, defeated. "What a fucking day.", I thought to myself. I did a systems check. What do I have left? I have my wallet, which is good. I have a blanket and a towel. I have Kristy's bike, but my keys were in the backpack! Damn it all to hell and back.

No house keys and I also couldn't take the bike with me because I had locked the front tire to the frame with a chain lock, and now the key was gone. Of course, I could have carried the bike the entire way back to the station, but I estimated it was at least two miles that we covered on the way there and that is a long way to carry even a light bike; which this bike was not. Not only that, but my shirt was tucked in my bag, too! At least I had my wallet, but still, this was a really stupid situation.

I picked up the bike and pushed it as far into the thicket as I could, rolled up the blanket, and with the towel around my neck, started walking back to civilization.

You can not imagine the amount of courage it took me to walk across that field of cows alone.

I made it back to the small parking lot, where there were some people getting out of their car that I asked how to get to the train station. They explained that I basically just needed to follow the road and turn right at the round-a-bout. It ended up being pretty straightforward, (except for the round-a-bout, of course.)

The way Bart took us was much more scenic, but it actually wasn't that hard to find after having been there once. I made it to the train station and luckily had my wallet so I could buy a ticket and didn't have to sneak on. However, I was still in a semi-wet bathing suit and had no shirt!

With all that had happened that day, this was probably the worst part. Yes, Germans will sit around with their schwaenze hanging out at the beach, but you will basically never see someone without a shirt on unless it's in a place designated for sunbathing or swimming.

Even on the hottest of days, it is not "normal" for a guy to walk down the street in the city without a shirt on. But there I was, sitting in a train with no shirt on. I walked all the way to the back of a car until I found a group of 4 seats where only one person was sitting. When I sat down, (with my towel around my shoulders and my blanket under my arm), the woman who was sitting there immediately stood up and walked away.

The closer we got back into the city, the more crowded the train became, but no one sat next to me the entire ride. I realised this is what homeless people must deal with on a daily basis. It made me so sad to think what daily life must be like for them. People looked at me with disgust, just because I was sitting there shirtless.

At one point, I made eye contact with a guy in a suit who entered the train and then hesitated as he walked past me. In frustration, I blurted out, "Ya, someone stole my stuff. How's your day going?" He walked by.

I decided to exit the train at the Hamburg main station because I figured taking a cab from there would be quicker and include less judgemental looks. I approached the first cab in the row and bent down to talk to the driver through the open passenger window.

In English, I said, "Hi, I know how this looks, but I'm fine. I was swimming and someone stole my stuff. Would you be kind enough to take me to the Operettenhaus?" I asked in English, figuring I might get some sympathy points if he also thought I was a tourist.

"You got money?", he asked, fairly.

I flashed my wallet.

"Get in the back." He said.

When I showed up at the stage door, the security guard was like, "Oh my God. Get in here. What are you doing walking around like that?"

"Girl, you will not believe how my day has been going…", I said.

Before the show, I called my building manager to tell her I got robbed and that I needed new keys. She was very helpful and explained how important it was that we keep it on the down-low because the building owner would freak out if she knew there was a set of keys missing. I was very thankful for her advice and willingness to un-officially help me, and I picked the keys up on my way home from work wearing my bathing suit and a t-shirt from the costume storage backstage.

After trudging up the 5 flights of stairs to my "penthouse apartment" overlooking the roofs of Hamburg's St. Pauli neighbourhood, I opened the door to find 2 messages on my answering machine; both from Bart.

"Hi Morgan, it's me. I just got home from the lake and I want you to know I am very disappointed in you. I'm… I'm furious. I thought we had a bright future, but apparently you were just playing with me. You sent me mixed signals and made me build up expectations and now it's all messed up. Anyways. I need some time to think about `us´ and, I know this will be hard for you, but please DO NOT call me or try to contact me in any way."

The second message was from a few hours later, this one with much more anger.

"Hi Morgan, it's Bart. Apparently I'm not even worth getting a phone call back. So I want you to know that I am erasing your number from my phone and erasing you from my life. I hope I never see you again. Goodbye!"

There were a lot of lessons learned that day. Don't leave your valuables completely unattended in the middle of the woods where you think no other soul could possibly find them. Be nice to people less fortunate, even if they are dressed inappropriately. Don't go out on a second date with someone who serves steamed artichoke as a main dish.

Stitches on a Cruise

The first words I mentioned when I saw the turquoise waters of Magen's Bay on the island of Saint Thomas were not, "Amazing!", or "It's beautiful!", but rather, "Damn it!" The moment my toes hit that warm sand, I realised I had forgotten something very important.

It was 2016 and at that time in my travel career, I was still an obsessive planner. I had known for months that this was the beach I wanted to visit on the island. I had a plan! When I got to the beach, I was going to buy some snacks from the small bar and then "turn right" to go all the way over to the end. That's where several reviews had recommended the most privacy and the best underwater life. I was going to spread out my towel and take my first GoPro camera out into the water to film the rays.

This beach was on Saint Thomas, one of the Virgin Islands, (they don't check before you arrive, in case you're worried about being denied entry). I arrived there on the Harmony of the Seas, which was the largest cruise ship at the time. It's basically a floating city with different neighbourhoods and real trees.

Not only was this my first time cruising without Markus, but so many things about this ship were firsts for me. First time on a current record holder, (which was only about 6 feet longer than the previous biggest ship in the world.) First time solo. First time in a cabin with a "virtual balcony."

When you arrive in the port on Saint Thomas, it's just a short walk to the taxi stand. "Taxi" is a confusing description of the vehicles because they are all, in fact, small busses or jeep-like things, many with open sides. The stands are set up with signs for the most popular destinations. You get in line at the stand and when the next vehicle comes, you pack in like sardines. You and 15 other strangers are carted to wherever you're going for a flat fee. (I have no idea how they're doing it during the current situation, but that's how it was last time I was there!)

When our vehicle arrived at the famous beach, which is also a national park, I had my camera out to record what the entry was like. A park worker boarded the bus and a millisecond afterwards called out to me, "Ey, are you taking my picture?"

"I'm recording the experience of getting to the beach to show my friends.", I replied.

"Gimme that card. You can not record people without their permission here. You did not ask me so I need to take that card.", she commanded.

I mean, this woman had literally just entered the vehicle. She walked in and immediately started looking for people with cameras that she could yell at. Her actual job was to collect $5 from every passenger for the park entrance. But her true passion was taking people's SD cards. I was not having it.

"I'll erase the picture, but I am not giving you the card," I said.

"Do you understand me?" she asked, slightly more aggressively. "You can not take pictures of people without their permission here. It's very disrespectful. I need to take that card."

"Listen,", I tried to sound friendly, „I really wasn't trying to take a picture of just you. I had my camera out to record this whole area," I pointed towards the beach with my hand, "and then you entered the jeep. You are not the focus of this video and I really mean no disrespect, but I can not give you the card out of this camera. Look, I'll just delete the entire video and then it's over."

Keep in mind, this was happening while everyone else in the jeep waited. I really feel like this was something this young woman did in every vehicle that arrived. What did she do with the SD cards that she actually got? Peruse people's vacation pictures? Sell them on eBay? She was working for the park, which basically makes her a government worker, doesn't it? Horrible. Anyways, I pretended to delete the video, (which I would have ACTUALLY done if it was possible, but on GoPros back then, there was no screen!) I had to pretend, but I guess she realised I was not going to let her scam me and decided to move on to her actual job.

After that whole fiasco was resolved, I continued with my plan of visiting the snack bar and purchasing a slice of pizza and a beer, (a Corona, incidentally,) and made my way down the beach.

Once I got to the end, I decided I wanted to get some wider shots of the beach itself. The long side of the bay is covered with larger rocks that disappear into the waterline, but. I was prepared for that. In fact, I saw some people sunbathing out on the rocks and thought that would be a cool place to plop my towel down for the day, so I slipped out of my street shoes and plopped my backpack down on the sand to get out my water shoes in preparation for wading out to the rocks.

"Damn it." I exclaimed, under my breath. I looked inside my backpack and quickly realised I had forgotten the water shoes. The water shoes I had purchased SPECIFICALLY for my visit to this beach!

I was so disappointed. It was one of those moments in life where you ask yourself, "How can you be so stupid?", like when you go to the grocery store for one important ingredient and then make it home with an entire bag of food, but not that ingredient.

I assessed the situation. There were quite a few people in the water and most of them did not have any protective covering on their feet. Big kids, little kids, it seemed like most people were doing just fine without. So, I picked up my street shoes, slung my backpack over one shoulder, and waded out into the water towards a group of rocks about 50 feet down the shore. I was looking forward to getting there, getting some great video footage, and popping open that ice cold beer.

It only took me about 15 steps before it happened. I was taking very slow, calculated steps, but with the small waves and the uneven surface of the sand underwater, I somehow managed to shortly lose my balance and had to take a few larger steps to avoid dumping my backpack into the water.

On one of those grand jetès through the waves, my foot came down hard on a rock. It felt really rough, but there was no pain. I was sure I had just scratched the skin and continued towards my destination. However, after a few more steps, I could tell something was going on with the skin under that foot and decided to take a detour to take a look.

Setting my bag down on one side and my shoes on the other, I sat my butt down on a warm rock and grabbed my ankle. There was a short, but very deep gash on the flat part between my pinky toe and its neighbour. A flap of skin about the size of a thumbnail was hanging off, but still firmly attached, and it was dark red underneath. And there was blood. It seemed like lots of blood to me. It dripped down the side of my foot onto the rock and there was quickly a small pool of red.

"Fuck." I whispered.

In the middle of this dramatic moment, I still managed to think of my creative duties as the producer of a travel show. I dug out my GoPro and pressed record. My reaction and thoughts over the next few minutes are on YouTube, but basically I realised after about 5 minutes that the bleeding was not stopping. Even though it didn't hurt whatsoever, I decided staying at the beach was probably not the best idea.

Figuring I could just go back to the ship and have someone in the medical center look at it, I made my way back. I was sure they would then probably laugh at me for making such a big deal out of such a small wound, slap a waterproof bandage on it, and in a few hours I would be back on the beach. In fact, I was so sure I was coming back that I buried my beer under a rock and noted the location so I could pick it up later.

Knowing sharks can smell blood underwater, I opted to sacrifice my dry shoes and just put them on, socks and all, for the trudge back to shore. Otherwise I was sure to get attacked by a shark in the 2 feet of water between me and the beach, right? Ok, ok, it wasn't the most rational of thinking, but it also kept any smaller parasites from swimming into the open wound on my foot.

When I arrived back on the ship, my bad mood at that point got even worse as I realised the medical center was closed! It was inconceivable to me at the time, but when the ship is in port, the medical center team also gets time off.

"I could have just stayed at the beach!" I thought. Even though we had at least 6 more hours on port, the possibility of going to a doctor on land never occurred to me. There didn't seem to be any difference in sitting around with a bleeding gash in my foot at the beach or on the ship. I was really working myself into a funk about the whole thing. So, I went back up to my cabin, opened the drapes to let some (virtual) light in, and decided to try my own hand at first aid.

You know that scene in "The Shining" where a gigantic tidal wave of blood comes spilling down the hallway? (Sorry, SPOILER ALERT: There's a scene in "The Shining" where a gigantic tidal wave of blood comes spilling down a hallway.)

Anyways, that is what I was expecting when I took off my shoe. My mood at this moment would have me believing nothing but the worst possible outcome. Fortunately, it ended up being very unspectacular. I carefully peeled off the now stained sock and realised that the bleeding had almost completely stopped. Having the shoe and sock putting constant pressure on it must have helped?

The wound was much easier to inspect under these circumstances and I realised it really wasn't that bad at all, although it definitely was deep. The layers looked like sashimi tuna, and looking at the amount of sand trapped down inside made my blood pressure rise again.

I knew the sooner I got the sand out of there, the better, so I went into the shower, spread the skin out as far as I could without puking or passing out, and tried to use the hand-held shower head as a hydro-blaster. It wasn't the most comfortable thing to do, but I figured the more I could get out on my own, the less I would have to rely on the staff in the medical center to do it.

When the medical center finally opened, there were a few other passengers already waiting in line to be seen by the time I hobbled downstairs. I was surprised at how "normal" this facility seemed. The waiting room and the reception area had the same bland colors just like a doctor's office on land.

I checked in with my name and info and was given the option of seeing an RN for $70 or a doctor for $130. Food and some cocktails were included in my cruise package, but medical attention apparently was not. I decided to splurge on the doctor because the receptionist explained to me that, if I needed stitches, it would have to be the doctor doing it anyway. After a short examination by a nurse from New Zealand, the doctor, from Mexico, came into the room. He had a deep, booming voice, but spoke quietly and calming.

There were a few minutes of poking and pulling before he recommended that we go down the hall to the operating room. Yes, cruise ships have an operating room and I hope that you never get to see one. There was a much better light to get a more detailed look inside. As I took a seat on the operating table, I wondered how many times this area of the ship had been used. The ship had just been launched a few months earlier, so it was very likely that no one had been on this table yet. It made me happier to think that.

After taking another look, the doc explained, "It's very superficial and I don't think you're going to need stitches, but there is sand inside. We have to get that out, and it's going to hurt, so let me put some topical anesthetic on it."

He offered to give me some "real" anesthetic but explained that the poke of the needle and the feeling until it started working would probably be more uncomfortable than just doing it without. He began digging and I began cringing.

"Sorry, it's going to hurt," he said.

"That's ok. You do what you have to do and I'll try not to scream.", I said.

"Ouch ouch ouch ouch ouch ouch."

"Sorry."

"It's ok." I managed through gritted teeth, "Ouch ouch ouuuuuuuuuch."

"Ok, it's deeper than I thought and there is a lot of sand in there so I'm going to give you the anesthetic because otherwise I'm really going to hurt you. You can scream or shout or do whatever you have to do."

"Anesthesia sounds expensive.", I said. My sense of humor often pipes up at the wrong time.

"You want me to do it without?", he asked.

"No, it's ok, but I better stop watching," I managed, starting to feel somewhat light headed.

As he jabbed a needle that felt like the size of a felt tipped pen into my foot, I seriously wanted to scream. The worst part about the whole thing is: it didn't work. I still felt every second of the process of him putting two stitches into my skin! If you watch the video now, you can see my breathing getting shallower and shallower as he sewed up my foot.

"Remember, the anesthetic is only so you don't feel the pain. You'll still feel me working in it," he said. But I swear I felt pain as well as pressure.

After a few minutes, he bandaged me up and sent me on my way, asking me to make sure I didn't get it wet. He also told me to come back in 2 days so he could check it, free of charge. I spent the rest of the day letting the robotic bartender mix me drinks, which kept my mind off the impending medical bill that was to be delivered to my cabin later that evening. In the end, it cost around $300. Cheaper than going to an ER on land in America, right?

The next day, we stopped on Saint Martin, where I had been looking forward to visiting the infamous airport beach. If you visit, you get to watch the planes land and take off while blasting sand and vacationers across the road. The second stop was to be the sandy paradise known as Orient Beach.

Keeping in mind what the doc said about not getting my foot wet, I made a bee-line for the first touristy supermarket, where I purchased some waterproof bandages and a pack of Magnum EXTRA LARGE condoms. (Ahem, not the first time in my life - wink wink, nudge nudge).

I sat down on a sun chair at the beach, slapped a bandage over the stitches, and then put two of the condoms over it like a sock. I was sure they would split, but dang, those things sure hold out under stress! After that, I happily put on my water shoes, (yes, I remembered to pack them this time), which hid most of the madness, and went swimming out into the fantastic, turquoise waters of Orient Bay.

After Thoughts

Truth

I mentioned that I sometimes don't tell the truth about my job when people ask me. In that case, I usually just say I'm a "video editor" or "producer". That sounds way less exciting and doesn't usually result in the entire interview. I've toyed with the idea of just telling everyone I'm a proctologist. I would imagine not many people ask a lot of questions about that line of work.

Water Shoes

Since slicing my foot open, my track record for remembering to bring my water shoes with me to beaches is embarrassingly low. Also, I've often wondered if anyone found that can of Corona I stashed under the rock at Magen's Bay. If it was you: you're welcome!

Stomach Aches

Remember the weird stomach aches I was getting? The ones I thought were from the stress of trying to keep my body in shape for the "New York" musical? Actually, I had a cancerous tumour growing on my appendix! I just didn't know it yet. That was where the stomach aches were coming from. I went in for a successful surgery the next May and have been cancer-free since.

David

Not only have I been lucky enough to see my idol David Copperfield live on stage a few times, but David has actually seen ME live onstage, too! He and his manager came to see "Grease!" in Düsseldorf while they were in town visiting Claudia Schiffer's family.

After the first big number, we came offstage for our costume change and other members of the cast were talking about it. I thought they were pulling my leg, but there he was sitting on the aisle of row 11! He came backstage during the intermission and I was starstruck. I couldn't bring myself to talk to him until our 5 minute call! The picture I have of us together is one of my most prized possessions. Now that it's possible again, I hope to visit his show in Vegas and get him to sign it for me.

Penthouse
Calling my apartment in Hamburg back then a "penthouse" makes it sound way more luxurious than it actually was. Yes, it was the top floor of the building. But it was a 5 floor walk-up, which was everything but luxurious. We had some truly memorable cast parties in that place because it was so close to the theater. I miss living there! When Markus and I were moving back to Hamburg after "MammaMia! - Berlin" finished, I called the super to ask if the place was available. Sadly, it wasn't. It wouldn't have been big enough for the both of us, anyways.

Lake
After that day with Bart, I moved on with my life and dating very quickly and basically forgot about him the way you do when you are single and playing the field.

That fall, Joe, a friend of mine from high school, came to Germany for a visit. We hadn't seen each other in about 5 years and had a lot of catching up to do. I took a few days off and we travelled around Europe, visiting Oktoberfest, Neuschwanstein Castle, and Copenhagen.

Of course I told him the story of Bart. On the spot, Joe coined the phrase "Bart the Bunny Boiler" as a nod to Glenn Close's character in "Fatal Instinct."

Before telling Joe the story, I hadn't thought about Bart in several months.

When we got back to Hamburg from our trip, mysteriously there was a message from him on my machine! Out of the blue! It was like he felt me talking about him, or something. Weird. His message said,

"Hi Morgan. It's Bart. I just wanted to let you know that I've had enough time to calm down and think about it, and that I would be willing to give you a second chance. Give me a call."

Joe dared me to do it, but I decided not to.

I went back a few days later to try to rescue my friend's bike at the lake. Of course it was gone. She was really cool about it, though.

I've been back to that lake many times but, like a lot of great secret things, everyone knows about it now and it's gotten very crowded.

Fancy Suit
I still have the custom tailored pin-striped suit I wore to the Magic Castle hanging in my closet. Somehow it shrunk 2 sizes even though I only had it dry cleaned! Isn't that strange? As I write this, Kolli and his family were just visiting us last weekend. I hand-me-downed another suit I bought at the same time to Kolli's oldest son. It fit him perfectly. He's twelve.

Printed in Great Britain
by Amazon

32702051R00057